ENERGY - A SCIENTIFIC, TECHNICAL AND
SOCIO-ECONOMIC BIBLIOGRAPHY


by


Kitty Hsieh


Bibliographic Series Number 12


Corvallis: Oregon State University Press

(c) 1976 Oregon State University Press

ISBN: 0-87071-132-6

TABLE OF CONTENTS

|  | pg. |
|---|---|
| Acknowledgment | ix |
| What and How | xi |
| I. General Energy Information | 1 |
|     Abstracts and Indexes | 1 |
|     Bibliographies | 1 |
|     Dictionaries | 2 |
|     Directories | 2 |
|     Statistics | 2 |
|     Selected List of Periodicals | 4 |
|     Selected Reading Materials | 5 |
| II. Specific Sources of Energy | 8 |
|     A. Coal | 8 |
|         Abstracts and Indexes | 8 |
|         Bibliographies | 8 |
|         Statistics | 8 |
|         Selected List of Periodicals | 9 |
|         Selected Reading Materials | 9 |
|     B. Mineral Resources | 10 |
|         Abstracts and Indexes | 10 |
|         Bibliographies | 10 |
|         Statistics | 11 |
|         Selected Reading Materials | 11 |
|     C. Natural Gas | 12 |
|         Abstracts and Indexes | 12 |
|         Bibliographies | 12 |
|         Statistics | 12 |
|         Selected List of Periodicals | 13 |

|       | D. Petroleum                          | 14 |
|-------|---------------------------------------|----|
|       | Abstracts and Indexes                 | 14 |
|       | Bibliographies                        | 14 |
|       | Directories                           | 14 |
|       | Statistics                            | 15 |
|       | Selected List of Periodicals          | 16 |
|       | Selected Reading Materials            | 17 |
| III.  | Specific Types of Energy              | 20 |
|       | A. Geothermal                         | 20 |
|       | Bibliographies                        | 20 |
|       | Directories                           | 20 |
|       | Statistics                            | 20 |
|       | Selected List of Periodicals          | 21 |
|       | Selected Reading Materials            | 21 |
|       | B. Hydroelectric                      | 23 |
|       | Bibliographies                        | 23 |
|       | Statistics                            | 23 |
|       | Selected List of Periodicals          | 23 |
|       | Selected Reading Materials            | 24 |
|       | C. Hydrogen and Synthetic Fuels       | 25 |
|       | Abstracts and Indexes                 | 25 |
|       | Selected List of Periodicals          | 25 |
|       | Selected Reading Materials            | 25 |
|       | D. Nuclear                            | 27 |
|       | Abstracts and Indexes                 | 27 |
|       | Bibliographies                        | 27 |
|       | Directories                           | 28 |
|       | Statistics                            | 28 |
|       | Selected List of Periodicals          | 29 |
|       | Selected Reading Materials            | 31 |
|       | E. Solar                              | 32 |
|       | Bibliographies                        | 32 |
|       | Directories                           | 32 |
|       | Statistics                            | 33 |
|       | Selected List of Periodicals          | 33 |
|       | Selected Reading Materials            | 34 |
|       | F. Tidal and Ocean Thermal            | 37 |
|       | Abstracts and Indexes                 | 37 |
|       | Statistics                            | 37 |
|       | Selected Reading Materials            | 37 |

|     |     |                                      | Page |
| --- | --- | ------------------------------------ | ---- |
|     | G.  | Wind                                 | 38   |
|     |     | Bibliographies                       | 38   |
|     |     | Selected Reading Materials           | 38   |
| IV. | Energy Related Topics |                    | 40   |
|     | A.  | Agriculture and Food Supply          | 40   |
|     |     | Abstracts and Indexes                | 40   |
|     |     | Bibliographies                       | 40   |
|     |     | Statistics                           | 40   |
|     |     | Selected List of Periodicals         | 41   |
|     |     | Selected Reading Materials           | 41   |
|     | B.  | Business and Economics               | 44   |
|     |     | Abstracts and Indexes                | 44   |
|     |     | Bibliographies                       | 44   |
|     |     | Statistics                           | 44   |
|     |     | Selected List of Periodicals         | 45   |
|     |     | Selected Reading Materials           | 46   |
|     | C.  | Conservation                         | 48   |
|     |     | Bibliographies                       | 48   |
|     |     | Directories                          | 48   |
|     |     | Statistics                           | 48   |
|     |     | Selected List of Periodicals         | 48   |
|     |     | Selected Reading Materials           | 49   |
|     | D.  | Education                            | 51   |
|     |     | Abstracts and Indexes                | 51   |
|     |     | Dictionaries                         | 51   |
|     |     | Selected List of Periodicals         | 51   |
|     |     | Selected Reading Materials           | 51   |
|     | E.  | Electricity                          | 52   |
|     |     | Abstracts and Indexes                | 52   |
|     |     | Statistics                           | 52   |
|     |     | Selected List of Periodicals         | 55   |
|     |     | Selected Reading Materials           | 56   |
|     | F.  | Environment                          | 57   |
|     |     | Abstracts and Indexes                | 57   |
|     |     | Bibliographies                       | 57   |
|     |     | Directories                          | 58   |
|     |     | Selected List of Periodicals         | 58   |
|     |     | Selected Reading Materials           | 59   |

G. Forestry . . . . . . . . . . . . . . . . . . . . . 61
    Statistics. . . . . . . . . . . . . . . . . . . . 61
    Selected List of Periodicals. . . . . . . . . . . 61
    Selected Reading Materials. . . . . . . . . . . . 61

H. Gross National Product . . . . . . . . . . . . . . 63
    Statistics . . . . . . . . . . . . . . . . . . . 63

I. Home & Housing . . . . . . . . . . . . . . . . . . 64
    Statistics . . . . . . . . . . . . . . . . . . . 64
    Selected List of Periodicals . . . . . . . . . . 64
    Selected Reading Materials. . . . . . . . . . . . 65

J. Policy and Politics . . . . . . . . . . . . . . . 67
    Abstracts and Indexes . . . . . . . . . . . . . . 67
    Directories . . . . . . . . . . . . . . . . . . . 67
    Selected List of Periodicals . . . . . . . . . . 68
    Selected Reading Materials . . . . . . . . . . . 69

K. Population . . . . . . . . . . . . . . . . . . . . 71
    Abstracts and Indexes . . . . . . . . . . . . . . 71
    Statistics . . . . . . . . . . . . . . . . . . . 71

L. Social-Science . . . . . . . . . . . . . . . . . . 72
    Abstracts and Indexes . . . . . . . . . . . . . . 72
    Bibliographies . . . . . . . . . . . . . . . . . 72
    Selected List of Periodicals . . . . . . . . . . 72
    Selected Reading Materials . . . . . . . . . . . 73

M. Technology . . . . . . . . . . . . . . . . . . . . 74
    Abstracts and Indexes . . . . . . . . . . . . . . 74
    Bibliographies . . . . . . . . . . . . . . . . . 74
    Selected List of Periodicals . . . . . . . . . . 75
    Selected Reading Materials . . . . . . . . . . . 76

N. Transportation . . . . . . . . . . . . . . . . . . 77
    Abstracts and Indexes . . . . . . . . . . . . . . 77
    Bibliographies . . . . . . . . . . . . . . . . . 77
    Statistics . . . . . . . . . . . . . . . . . . . 78
    Selected List of Periodicals . . . . . . . . . . 78
    Selected Reading Materials . . . . . . . . . . . 79

O. Waste Recycling . . . . . . . . . . . . . . . . . 80
    Bibliographies . . . . . . . . . . . . . . . . . 80
    Selected List of Periodicals . . . . . . . . . . 80
    Selected Reading Materials . . . . . . . . . . . 81

Appendix I. . . . . . . . . . . . . . . . . . . . . . . .  83

       Selected Energy Publications on Oregon and
       the Pacific Northwest. . . . . . . . . . . . .  83

Appendix II. . . . . . . . . . . . . . . . . . . . . . .  85

       Selected Energy Publications from Oregon
       State University. . . . . . . . . . . . . . .  85

Index  . . . . . . . . . . . . . . . . . . . . . . . . .  88

ACKNOWLEDGMENT

This research was made possible through financial support from the Office of the Dean of Research and the Office of Energy Research and Development, Oregon State University, the unfailing assistance of Ms. Debbie Steckly, and contribution of information and ideas of staff members from the Social Science/Humanities and the Science/Technology Divisions of the Oregon State University Library.

Kitty Hsieh

September 1976

## WHAT AND HOW

This bibliography is prepared for researchers in various fields of energy, teachers and students at the college level or above, and whoever helps the above people with their research or teaching.

Emphasis is placed on users of the Oregon State University Library, hence a call number (in parenthesis) is given after every item in the OSU Library to assist users in locating the item. Special effort is made to sort out publications on Oregon and the Pacific Northwest and by researchers at OSU (see Appendix I, II).

The following explanation of notations in this bibliography is for the OSU Library users only:

1. To look for an item without a call number:
   a. Look in the Library Card Catalog and see if the Library has received the item since the compilation of this bibliography.
   b. Ask at the Science-Technology Desk, 5th floor, to see if the item is on the "Energy Shelf"

2. "R" after a call number means the item is in the reference area of the Social Science and Humanities Division, 2nd floor. "R Sci.Tech." after a call number means the item is in the reference area of the Science-Technology Division, 5th floor.

3. An item with a plain "Z" call number is on the 4th floor, while an item with the term "Sci.Tech" after the "Z" is on the 5th floor.

4. A dash sign "-" after the date of publication of an item means this is a continuous publication. It can be a journal or a series.

Users of this bibliography are encouraged to consult <u>Energy Referenc Sources</u> (by Kitty Hsieh, 1975) for additional <u>information</u>.

# I. GENERAL ENERGY INFORMATION

## Abstracts and Indexes

1. ERDA Energy research Abstracts. U.S. Energy Research and Development Administration. (TJ163 U5 R Sci. Tech.)

2. Energy: A Key--Phrase Dissertation Index. (To be published Sept. 1976) University Microfilms International.

3. Energy Abstracts. Engineering Index, Inc., New York.

4. Energy Index. Environment Information Center, Inc., Energy Reference Dept., (TJ153 E55 R Sci.Tech.)

5. Energy Information abstracts. New York, Environment Information Center.(TJ163 .2 E52 R Sci. Tech.)

6. Energy Films Catalog. U.S. ERDA. 1976.

7. Energy Review. Energy Research Corporation, Santa Barbara, California.

8. Weekly Government Abstracts: Energy. National Technical Information Service, Springfield, Va.

## Bibliography

1. Alternate Sources of Energy: a Bibliography of Solar, Geothermal, Wind, and Tidal Energy, and Environmental Architecture. Barbara & David Harrah. (TJ163 .2 H2) 1975.

2. Energy. A Special Bibliography with Indexes. National Aeronautics and Space Administration. 1974. (TL521 A54088l no. 7042 R Sci.Tech.)

3. Energy,Continuing Bibliography with Indexes. National Aeronautics and Space Administration. (TL 521 A54088l no.71431 R Sci.Tech.)

4. Energy Reference Sources. Kitty Hsieh.(TJ153 O75 R Sci.Tech)1975.

5. Energy Research and Technology; Abstracts of NSF/RANN Research Reports. United States. National Science Foundation. (Q180 U5 U543 R Sci.Tech.) 1975.

6. Energy Research and Development: a Selected Reading List. National Technical Information Service, Springfield, Va. 1973. ORNL-EIS-73-65.

7. Energy Supply and Demand and the Availability of Energy Sources; a Bibliography with Abstracts. By Edward J. Lehmann. (HD9502 U52 L4)

8. Selected Sources of Information on US and World Energy Resources. US Geological Survey Circular #641. 1970. (QE75 C5 #641)

9. Information Sources in Power Engineering. By Karen S. Metz. (TJ163.2 M48)

10. Technical Reports of the Federal Energy Administration. U.S. FEA. 1976. (PB 248-915) NTIS.

Dictionaries

1. Energy Reference Handbook. Government Institute, 1974. Ed. N.C. McNerney and Thomas Sullivan. (TJ153 E58 R Sci.Tech.)

2. A Guide to Energy Related Terms. Oregon Office of Energy Research and Development. 1975. (TJ9 07 R Sci.Tech.)

Directories

1. Directory of Federal Energy Data Sources: Computer Products and Recurring Publications. 1976. U.S. FEA. (PB 254-163) NTIS.

2. Directory of State Government Energy-Related Agencies. 1975. National Energy Information Center. (TJ163.3 A2 D5 R Sci.Tech.)

3. Energy Directory. Environment Information Center, Inc. 1974-. Annual. (TJ153 E54 R Sci.Tech.)

4. Energy Information Resources. An Inventory of Energy Research and Development Information Resources in the Continental U.S., Hawaii and Alaska. American Society for Information Science. 1975. (TJ163.25 U6 B37 1975 R Sci.Tech.)

5. Energy Information in the Federal Government. A Directory of Energy Sources Identified by the Interagency Task Force on Energy Information. 1975. (PB 246-703). (HD9502 U52 E486)

6. Information on International Research and Development Activities in the Field of Energy. By David F. Hersey. 1976. (NSF/RA-760057)

7. Information Sources in Power Engineering. By Karen S. Metz. 1975. (TJ163.2 M48)

Statistics

1.  Energy Information. Quarterly. U.S. Federal Energy Administration. (HD9502 U52 U528)

2.  Energy Perspectives; A Presentation of Major Energy and Energy Related Data. U.S. Department of the Interior. 1975. (HD9502 U52 U525 R)

3.  Energy Resources of the United States. US Geological Survey Circular #650. 1972. (QE75 C5 #650)

4.  Energy Statistics. U. S. Senate. Committee on Finance. Committee Print. 1975.

5.  Energy Statistics: A Guide to Sources. By S. Balachandran. (Z7164 O7 C6 #1065). Council of Planning Librarians Exchange Bibliography #1065, June 1976.

6.  Monthly Bulletin of Statistics. UN Statistical Office. 1947-. (HC59 U7)

7.  Monthly Energy Review. National Energy Information Center. 1975- . (HD9502 U52 M6)

8.  Statistical Yearbook. UN Statistical Office. 1948- . (HA12.5 U6 R)

9.  Patterns of Energy Consumption in the United States. By Stanford Research Institute. 1972. (HD9545 S7)

10. Project Independence Blueprint: Transcript of Public Hearings. U.S. FEA. (HD9502 U52 U53) 1974.

11. National Power Survey. U.S. Federal Power Commission. 1964- . (HD9685 U5 A23)

12. Power Series. U.S. Federal Power Commission. (TJ23 A52)

13. Statistical Papers. Series J: Energy. UN Statistical Office. 1966- . (TJ153 U6)

14. Survey of Energy Resources. World Energy Conference. U. S. National Committee of the World Energy Conference. 1962- . (HD9502 A2 W6 R)

15. United States Energy Fact Sheets By States and Regions. U.S. Dept. of the Interior. 1973- . (HD9544 A35)

16. United States Energy Through the Year 2000. By Walter G. Dupree and James A. West. U.S. Dept. of the Interior. 1972- . (HD9545 D83)

17. World Energy Resources. 1975. U.S. ERDA-53. (TJ153 U535)

18. World Energy Supplies. 1950-1974. U.N. Statistical Office. Statistical Papers Ser. J. no.19. (TJ153 U6) 1976.

Selected List of Periodicals

1. Annual Review of Energy. Palo Alto, Calif. 1976- . (TJ163 .2 A55)

2. Energy Information. Weekly.

3. Energy International. Monthly. (TJ1 E47)

4. Energy Perspectives. Monthly. (By Battelle Memorial Institute)

5. Energy R & D Conference. Proceedings. Government Institutes. (HD9545 E63)

6. Energy Sources. Quarterly.

7. Energy World. Monthly. (TP315 E5)

8. Science. (Q1 S32)

9. Energy Users Report. (HD9540 E51 R)

10. Science News. (Q1 S34)

11. Scientific American. (Q1 S357)

12. Energy, an International Journal. Monthly.

12. ERDA. U.S. Energy Research and Development Administration. (TJ153 U535)

13. Energy Information Reported to Congress as Required by Public Law 93-319. (HD9502 U52 U528) U.S. FEA.

14. Research Applied to National Needs Program. NSF-RA-N series. (Q180 U5 U54)

15. World Energy Conference. Transactions. (TJ5 W6)

G. Selected Reading Materials.

1. Conference on Magnitude and Deployment Schedule of Energy Resources. Proceedings.(HD9502 U52 C7 1975)

2. Conference on Cooperation in Energy Information. Arlington, VA. 1975. (HD9502 U52 C665)

3. Economic and Technical Feasibility Study for Energy Storage Flywheels. 1975. U.S. ERDA 76-65. (TJ153 U535)

4. Energy. Science Forum, Aug. 1975. (Q1 A1 S3)

5. Energy. Science. April 19, 1974. (Q1 S32)

6. Energy. By Gerard M. Crawley. 1975. (TJ153 C7)

7. Energy. By S.S. Penner and L. Icerman. v.1. Demands, Resources impact, technology, and policy. v.2. Non-Nuclear Energy Technologies. v.3. Nuclear Energy and Energy Policies. (HD9502 A2 P46) 1974.

8. Energy: Resource, Slave, Pollutant; A Physical Science Text. By Robert S. Rouse, and Robert O. Smith.

9. Energy Atlas of Asia and the Far East. United Nations. Economic Commission for Asia and the Far East. (G2201 N3 U5 1970 R Map Room)

10. Energy Crisis Handbook. Ed. by Howard Gordon. 1976.

11. Energy Crisis in Perspective. By John C. Fisher. (HD9540 .6 F57) 1974.

12. Energy for Survival; The Alternative to Extinction. By Wilson Clark. (TJ153 C53) 1974.

13. Energy for Tomorrow. By Philip H. Abelson. (HD9502 U52 A2)

14. Energy History of the U.S. 1776-1976. U.S. ERDA. 1975

15. Energy in Europe, 1945-1980. By W. G. Jensen. (HD9555 A5 J4)

16. Energy in Perspective. By Jerry B. Marion. (HD9502 U52 M375)

17. Energy Modeling: Art, Science, Practice. By Milton F. Searl.

18. Energy Resources. (The Open Univ.)

19. Energy Research Needs. By Sam H. Schurr. (HD9545 S32)

20. Energy Research Program of the U.S. Department of the Interior. U.S. Dept. of the Interior. 1974. (TJ153 A3)

21. Future Energies. By Roy Meador.

22. International Conference on Energy. Europe and the 1980's. Papers. IEE Conference Publication Series No.112. 1974. (TK1 I495)

23. Inventory of Current Energy Research and Development. U.S. House. 93rd Congress. 1st Session Committee Print. 1973.

24. A National Plan for Energy Research Development and Demonstration. 1975. U.S. ERDA-48. (TJ153 U535)

25. A National Plan for Energy Research Development and Demonstration: Creating Energy Choices for the Future. 1976. U.S. ERDA-76-1. (TJ153 U535)

26. National Power Survey: Energy Sources Research; Report to the Technical Advisory Committee on Research and Development. U.S. Federal Power Commission. (HD9502 U52 U55) 1974.

27. New Energy: Understanding the Crisis and a Guide to an Alternative Energy System. By James Ridgeway and Bettina Conner. (HD9502 U52 R53) 1975.

28. National Energy Data Workshop. Proceedings of the National Energy Data Workshop. 1974 Purdue University. (HD9502 U52 N34 1974)

29. National Power Survey: Power Generation: Conservation, Health, and Fuel Supply; Report and Recommendations.1975. U.S. Fedaral Power Commission. Task Force on Conservation and Fuel Supply. (HD9502 U52 U54)

30. An Overview of Energy and Energy Related Research in the West. By. Walter J. Mead. 1975. (HD9502 U52 M4)

31. Resources (Renewable and Non-renewable). Science. Feb.20,1976 (Q1 S32)

32. Topics in Energy and Resources. Orbis Scientiae, University of Miami. 1974. (TJ153 O66 1974)

33. U.S. Energy Outlook; National Petroleum Council 1973- . (HD9502 U52 N373 1973)

34. The U.S. Energy Problem. By George Szego. 1976. 3 vol. (HD9502 U52 S9)

35. Energy Alternatives: A Comparative Analysis. By the Science and Public Policy Program. Univ. of Oklahoma. 1975. (TJ163 .25 U6 O35 1975)

36. National Energy Outlook. Annual. U.S. FEA. (HD9502 U52 N35)

## II. SPECIFIC SOURCES OF ENERGY

A. Coal

Abstracts and Indexes

1. National Coal Board Abstracts. England.
   Abstracts A: Technical Coal Press. Monthly.
   Abstracts B: Coal and Mining Geology. Bi-Monthly.

   See Also I.A, page 1.

Bibliographies

1. Classified List; Papers Published in the Journal of Fuel, and in Reports of Special Studies of the Institute. Institute of Fuel, London. Irregular. (TP315 I59)

Statistics

1. Bituminous Coal Facts. National Coal Association,. 1956- . Biennial. (HD9544 B472)

2. Coal Facts. Annual. National Coal Association. (HD9544 B472)

3. International Coal Trade. Monthly. U.S. Bureau of Mines. (HD9540 .4 U5)

4. Project Independence Task Force Report. Coal. 1974. U.S. FEA (HD9502 U52 P76)

5. Short-term Coal Forecast, 1975-1980. Federal Energy Administration. 1975. (TN805 A5 S5)

Selected Reading Materials

1. Coal Liquefaction. 1975-76. U.S. ERDA-76-33-3. (TJ153 U535)

2. Coal Management Techniques, 1st Symposium. National Coal Association, & Bituminous Coal Research Inc.

3. Coal Utilization, Symposium. National Coal Assoc. & Bituminous Coal Research Inc. (TD885 .5 S8 C6 1974 1st)

4. Cokemaking & Coal Gasification, Symposium of the Division of Fuel Chemistry at 170th meeting. American Chemical Society. 1975

5. Energy from Coal. Guidelines for the Preparation of Environmental Impact Statements. NTIS

6. Energy From Coal. U.S. ERDA 76-67. (TJ153 U535) 1976.

7. Fluidised Combustion Conference. Institute of Fuel. 1975.

8. Multicell Fuidized-bed Boiler Design, Construction and Test Program PB-236 254. 1974.

9. U.S. Coal and the Electric Power Industry. By Richard L. Gordon. 1975. (HD9502 U52 G67)

Selected List of Periodicals

1. Fuel; A Journal of Fuel Science. (TP315 F9)

2. Coal Age. (TN1 C6)

3. Journal. Institute of Fuel, Quarterly. (TP315 I6)

4. Research and Development Report. U.S. Office of Coal Research. (TP325 U65) Irregular.

B.  Mineral Resources.

Abstracts and Indexes

1. Nuclear Science Abstracts.  (for Nuclear Fuels)
   (QC173 N8 R Sci.Tech)

2. Weekly Government Abstracts: Natural Resources.  National Technical Information Service.

3. Abstracts of North American Geology.  1966-1970.  (QE71 A2 R Sci.Tech.)

   See Also I.A, page 1.


Bibliographies

1. Annotated Bibliography of Economic Geology.  Economic Geo-Pub. Co.  (Z6033 E4 Z2 R Sci.Tech.)  1928-65.

2. Bibliography of Literature Pertinent to Mining Reclamation in Arid and Semi-Arie Environments. By Gerald F. Gifford, Don D. Dwyer and Brien E. Norton.  1972.  (Z6738 R4 G4   SciTech)

3. Bibliography and Index of Geology.  Geological Society of America.  1933-   .  (Z6031 N5 R Sci. Tech)

4. List of Bureau of Mines Publications and Articles.  U.S. Bureau of Mines. 1960-   . (TN23 U651 R Sci. Tech.)

5. List of Publications Issued by the Bureau of Mines from July 1, 1910 to January 1, 1960.  U.S. Bureau of Mines. (TN23 U65 R   Sci. Tech.)

6. Index of Mining Engineering Literature, Comprising an Index of Mining, Metallurgical, Civil, Mechanical, Electrical and Chemical Engineering Subjects as Related to Mining Engineefing.  By Walter R. Crane.  1909-12.  (Z6737 C7 R Sci. Tech.)

7. The Mining World Index of Current Literature.  Mining World Co.  1912-1916.  (Z6737 M5 R. Sci. Tech.)

8. Bibliography of North American Geology.  U.S. Geological Survey.  1919-   .  (QE75 B9 R Sci. Tech.)  1919-70.

Statistics

1. Annual Report of the Secretary of the Interior Under the Mining and Minerals Policy Act of 1970. 1971-    . (TN23 U72)

2. Mineral Industry Surveys. Monthly and Annual. U.S. Bureau of Mines. (TN23 U588 R Sci. Tech)

3. Minerals Yearbook. 1933-   . U.S. Bureau of Mines. (TN23 U59 R  Sci. Tech.)

4. Uranium Resources, Production and Demand. IAEA and OECD Nuclear Energy Agency. 1973.

5. World Mineral and Energy Resources--some Facts and Assessments, 1974. (HD9506 A2 H3)

6. United States Mineral Resources; Ed. by Donald A. Brobst. Geological Survey. Professional Paper no. 820. (QE75 P7 no. 820) 1973.

7. World Resource Production: 50 Years of Change. By Harry V. Warren and F. F. Wilks. 1966. (G4 B7 no.5.)

8. Minerals in the U.S. Economy, Ten-Year Supply Demand Profile for Minerals and Fuel Commodities. U.S. Bureau of Mines. 1975. (HD9506 U62 Y54)


Selected Reading Materials

1. Affluence in Jeopardy; Minerals and the Political Economy. By. Charles F. Park. 1968. (HD9506 U62 P2)

2. Earthbound: Minerals, Energy, and Man's Future. By Charles F. Park. 1975. (HD9506 A2 P37 1975)

3. Mineral Resources and the Environment. National Research Council. 1975. (HD9506 A2 N3)

4. Politics, Minerals, and Survival. By Ralph W. Marsden. 1974. (HD9506 U62 P65)

C. Natural Gas

Abstracts and Indexes

    1. Gas Abstracts. Institute of Gas Technology. Monthly.

See also I.A, page 1.


Bibliographies

    1. A Century of Oil and Gas in Books, a Descriptive Bibliography. By Edward Benjamin Swanson. 1960. (Z6972 S9    Sci. Tech.)


Statistics

    1. Annual and Accrued Mineral Production, Royalty Income, and Related Statistics (Oil, Gas, and Other Leasable Minerals). U.S. Geological Survey, Division of Conservation, 1951- . (HD9506 U5 U5)

    2. The Future Supply of Oil and Gas; a Study of the Availability of Crude Oil, Natural Gas and Natural Gas Liquids in the U.S. in the Period Through 1975. By Bruce C. Netschert. 1958. (TN872 A5 N4)

    3. Gas Facts. American Gas Association, Dept. of Statistics. Arlington, Va. Annual. (TP722 A615)

    4. Gas Utility Statistics. Monthly. American Gas Association.

    5. Historical Statistics of the Gas Industry. American Gas Association, Bureau of Statistics. 1961. (TP722 A6)

    6. Indexes of Output Per Man-Hour Gas and Electric Utilities Industry, 1932-62. 1964. (HD9684 U6 A2)

    7. National Gas Survey. U.S. Federal Power Commission. 1971-75. 5 volumes. (HD9581 U5 U53 1974- )

8. Oil and Gas Resources, Reserves, and Productive Capacities. U.S. Federal Energy Administration. (TN872 A45 1975a)1975-

9. Project Independence Task Force Report. Natural Gas. U.S. FEA. 1974. (HD9502 U52 P76)

10. Reserves of Crude Oil, Natural Gas Liquids, and Natural Gas In the United States and Canada. American Gas Assoc., (TN872 A5 A63) Irregular.

11. Sales by Producers of Natural Gas to Interstate Pipeline Companies. U.S. Federal Power Commission, 1961- Biennial. (HD9581 U5 A3)

12. Statistics of Oil and Gas Development and Production. American Institute of Mining and Metallurgical Engineers, (TN872 A5 A65) Annual.

13. Utility Appropriations. The Conference Board, Quarterly. (HC101 N246)

Selected List of Periodicals

1. Annual Report; American Gas Association, PAR Committee. (TP700 A52)

2. Chilton's Oil and Gas Energy. Chilton Co., Monthly. 1975- (HD9560 .1 C5)

3. The Oil and Gas Journal. Weekly. (TN860 05)

4. Pipline and Gas Journal. (TP700 A53)

D. Petroleum

Abstracts and Indexes

1. API (American Petroleum Institute) Abstracts of Refining Literature. Petroleum Refining and Petrochemical Abstracts. Weekly.

2. International Petroleum Abstracts. Applied Science Publishers, England. Quarterly. (TN860 I52 R Sci. Tech.)

3. Petroleum Abstracts. Univ. of Tulsa, Oklahoma. Weekly.

See Also I.A, page 1.

Bibliographies

1. A Century of Oil and Gas in Books, a Descriptive Bibliography. 1960. (Z6972 S9  Sci. Tech.)

Directories

1. International Petroleum Encyclopedia. Petroleum Publishing co. (HD9560 .5 I59 R)

2. OPD Chemical Buyers Directory. Annual (TP12 O5 R Sci. Tech.)

3. The Petroleum Register.  M. Palmer. Annual. (TN867 P4)

## Statistics

1. American Association of Petroleum Geologists. Bulletin. June issue. (TN860 A5)

2. Annual and Accrued Mineral Production, Royalty Income, and Related Statistics (Oil, Gas, and Other Leasable Minerals). U.S. Giological Survey, Division of Conservation. (HD9506 U5 U5)

3. Bunker Fuels. United States. Bureau of the Census. (HD9560 .4 U47)

4. International Petroleum. Annual. U.S. Bureau of Mines. (HD9560 .2 U7)

5. National Petroleum Product Supply and Demand. Annual. U.S. FEA (HD9502 U52 U537 no.74-5, 75-5, etc.)

6. The Petroleum Almanac; a Statistical Record of the Petroleum Industry in the United States and Foreign Countries. Nattional Industrial Conference Board. 1946. (HD9560 .4 P4)

7. Oil and Gas Journal. Regular Weekly statistics and annual Directory and Forecast issues. (TN860 05)

8. Oil and Gas Resources, Reserves, and Productive Capacities. U.S. FEA. 1975 (TN872 A45 1975)

9. Petroleum Facts and Figures. American Petroleum Institute. 1953. 11th ed. (HD9565 A53)

10. Project Independence Task Force Report. Oil. U.S. FEA 1974. (HD9502 U52 P76)

11. Project Independence Task Force Report. Oil Shale. U.S. FEA. 1974. (HD9502 U52 P76)

12. Reserves of Crude Oil, Natural Gas Liquids, and Natural Gas in the United States and Canada. (TN872 A5 A63)

13. Statistics of Oil and Gas Development and Production. American Institute of Mining and Metallurgical Engineers. (TN872 A5 A65)

14. World Petroleum Report. M. Palmer. Annual. (HD9560 .4 W6)

15. Monthly Petroleum Statistics Report. U.S. FEA.

Selected List of Periodicals
1. American Association of Petroleum Geologists. Bulletin. 1917- . (TN860 A5)
2. American Petroleum Institute. Division of Refining. Proceedings. Annual. (TN860 A64)
3. Chilton's Oil and Gas Energy. Monthly. 1975- .(HD9560 .1 C5)
4. Energy Pipelines and Systems. (TP690 A1 E5) 1974.
5. Exxon USA. (HD9569 H9 A7)
6. Hydrocarbon Processing. (TP690 A1 P4)
7. Lamp. Quarterly. (HD9560 .1 L3)
8. Journal of Canadian Petroleum. (TN860 J58)
9. Journal of Petroleum Technology. (TN860 J6)
10. National Petroleum News, the National Oil Weekly. (TN860 N3)
11. Offshore. (TN871 .3 O27)
12. Our Sun. Sun Oil Co. Quarterly. (HD9569 S9 O9)
13. Oilweek. (HD9574 C2 O5)
14. The Oil and Gas Journal. (TN860 O5)
15. Oil Shale and Cannel Coal Conference. Proceedings. 1938- . The Institute of Petroleum, London. (TN863 O6)
16. Oilways. (TN860 H9)
17. Pacific Petroleum Geologist. 1947- . (TN860 P2)
18. Petroleum Age. 1921- . (HD9560 .1 P4)
19. Petroleum Engineer International. Monthly. (TN860 P33)
20. Petroleum Processing. (TP690 A1 P38) 1946- .
21. Petroleum Press Service. Petroleum Press Bureau. London. Monthly. (HD9560 .1 P47)

22. Petroleum Review. (TP690 Al P42)

23. Petroleum Today. American Petroleum Institute. (TN860 P42)

24. Pipeline Industry. (TJ930 P5)

25. Shell Oil Papers on the Energy Situation. 1973- .
    (TJ153 S4)

26. Society of Petroleum Engineers Journal. (TN860 S6)

27. Standard Oil Co. Report. Annual. (HD2769 S8 A3)

28. Western Oil and Refining. Review Number. (TN862 P4)

30. World Oil. (TN860 W57)

31. World Petroleum Congresses. Proceedings. (TN863 W6)


Selected Reading Materials

1. Cry Crisis!: Rehearsal in Alska. By Harvey Manning. 1974.
   (HD9502 U52 M37)

2. The Economic of Arctic Oil Transportation. By J. B. Lassiter.
   1970. GC4 MIT A2 no.71-4.

3. The Elusive Bonanza; The Story of Oil Shale--America's
   Richest and Most neglected Natural Resource. 1970.
   (HD9565 W47)

4. The Energy Cartel: Big Oil vs. The Public Interest. 1975.
   (HD9566 M43 1975) Norman Medvin.

5. The Energy Cartel: Who Runs the American Oil Industry.
   By Norman Medvin. 1974. (HD9566 M44 1974)

6. Energy Under the Oceans, A Technology Assessment of Outer
   Continental Shelf Oil and Gas Operations. By. D. E. Kash.
   1974.

7. Future Petroleum Provinces of the United States--Their Geology and Potential. Ed. by Ira H. Cram. (TN860 A53 v.15)

8. Highway Robbery: An Analysis of the Gasoline Crisis. By Fred C. Allvine and James M. Patterson. (HD9564 A79 1974)

9. Middle East Oil and the Energy Crisis. By Joe Stork. 1975.

10. Middle East Oil and U.S. Foreign Policy. By Shoshana Klebanoff. 1974. (HD9576 N36 K57)

11. Multinational Oil; A Study in Industrial Dynamincs. By Neil H. Jacoby. 1974. (HD9560 .5 J26)

12. Offshore Petroleum Transfer Systems for Washington State; A Feasibility Study. 1974. (HE199 .5 P4 W3)

13. Offshore Terminal System Concepts; Executive Summary. Soros Associates. 1972. (HE553 S6)

14. Petroleum Resources Under the Ocean Floor. National Petroleum Council. 1969. (TN872 A5 N33)

15. Oil and World Power. By Peter R. Odell. (HD9560 .5 O33 1974)

16. Oil Producers and Consumers: Conflict or Cooperation. 1974. (HD9560 .1 O5)

17. Oil Transportation by Tankers: An Analysis of Marine Pollution and Safety Measures. (K U43) 1975.

18. Optimum Use of World Petroleum. AICHE Symposium Series no.142. 1974. (TP1 A52)

19. Petroleum and the Continental Shelf of Northwest Europe. Ed. by Austin W. Woodland. (TN874 A1 P47) 1975- .

20. Petroleum Evaluations and Economic Decisions. By A.W. McGray. 1975.

21. Petroleum Pipelines and Public Policy, 1906-1959. By Arthur M. Johnson. 1967. (HD9580 U4 J6)

22. Petroleum Tax Policy and the Energy Gap. 1973. (HD9566 P43)

23. Petroleum Transportation Systems Study. U.S. Army Engineer Institute for Water Resources. 1975. (HE199 .5 P4 N3)

24. Power from the Sea; The Search for North Sea Oil and Gas. By Clive Callow. 1973. (TN871 .3 C34)

25. The Pricing of Crude Oil; Economic and Strategic Guidelines for an International Energy Policy. Taki Rifai. 1974. (HD9560 .6 R53)

26. Supership. By Noel Mostert. 1974. (VM395 A7 M67 1974)

27. The Transportation of North Slope Oil and Long-range Alaska Transport Needs. By Richard A. Rice. 1972. (HD213 A4 R5)

28. The Future of World Oil. By Paul L. Eckbo. 1976.

## III. SPECIFIC TYPES OF ENERGY

A. Geothermal

Bibliographies

1. Annotated and Indexed Bibliography of Geothermal Phenomena. By. W. Kelly Summers. 1971. (Z6033 T35 S8 R Sci. Tech.)

2. Geothermal Energy; A Bibliography with Abstracts. By Axel C. Ringe. 1974. (Z6033 T35 R5 R Sci. Tech.)

3. Geothermal Resources: Exploration and Exploitation. ERDA Bibliography Series. TID-3354.

    (For Abstracts and Indexes see I.A, page 1.)

Directories

1. Geothermal World Directory. 1972-   . (QE528 G4 R Sci.Tech.)

Statistics

1. Geothermal Energy. By Edward R. Berman. 1975.

2. Geothermal Energy; Resources, Production, Stimulation. Ed. by Paul Kruger and Carel Otte. 1973. (QE528 K7 1972)

3. Project Independence Task Force Report. Geothermal Energy. U.S. FEA. 1974. (HD9502 U52 P76)

Selected List of Periodicals

1.  Geothermal Energy Magazine. (TJ280 .7 G44)

2.  Geothermics.

3.  Geotimes. (QE1 G694)

4.  Geyser, The International Geothermal Energy Newsletter.

5.  Journal of Volcanology and Geothermal Research. (QE521.5 J6)


Selected Reading Materials

1.  Alvord Desert Geothermal Leasing Program. U.S. Bureau of Land Management. 1975. (TD194 .5 U53 no. 7)

2.  Assessment of Geothermal Resources of the U.S. 1975. U.S.G.S. Circular no. 726. (QE75 C5)

3.  Feasibility Study for Development of Hot Water Geothermal Systems. By Jim Combs. 1973.

4.  Geothermal Energy. By Edward R. Berman. 1975. Noyes Data Copr. (Energy Technolody Rev. no.4)

5.  Geothermal Energy. Scientific Laboratory. University of California. 1973. (GB1005 S6)

6.  Geothermal Energy: A National Proposal for Geothermal Resources Research. 1973. Alaska University Pub.

7.  Geothermal Energy and Colorado. A Symposium. 1974. Colorado Geological Survey. Bulletin no. 35. (QE91 A4)

8.  Geothermal Energy; Resources, Production Stimulation. Ed. by Paul Kruger and Carel Otte. 1973. (QE528 K7 1972)

9.  Geothermal Environmental Analysis Record, Surprise, Warner, and Long Valleys, California, Oregon, Nevada. 1975. (TD194 .5 U53 no. 9)

10. Geothermal Overviews of the Western United States. Geothermal Resources Council. 1972. (GB1021 G4)

11. The Geothermal Steam Story or a Hot Tip From Mother Earth. By Rudolph J. Birsic. 1974.(TK1041 B55)

12. Geothermics. By Jean Goguel. 1976.

13. Geothermics, With Special Reference to Application. By O. Kappelmeyer and R. Haenel. (TN269 G384 ser.1.no.4)1974.

14. Heat and Mass Transfer in the Earth: Hydrothermal Systems. By. J.W. Elder. 1966. (GB1179 E5)

15. Klamath Basin; Environmental Analysis Record for Proposed Geothermal Leasing. U.S. Bureau of Land Management. 1975. (TD194 .5 U53 no.13)

16. Multipurpose Use of Geothermal Energy. Proceedings of the International Conference on Geothermal Energy for Industrial, Agricultural, and Commerical - Residential Uses. 1974.

17. National Geothermal Conference. 1976. Proceedings.

18. Physical Volcanology. Ed. by L. Civetta. 1974. (QE522 P58)

19. Prospectives for Nuclear-Stimulated Geothermal Power in the Western U.S. Western Interstate Nuclear Board. 1973. (TK1041 S3)

20. Ranking Research Problems in Geothermal Development. 1975. By Alan Laird. Office of Saline Water Research and Development Progress Report no. 711. (TD479 U5 no.711)

21. Simulation of Geothermal Energy Resources. By Paul Kruger. U.S. ERDA-37. (TJ153 U535)1975.

22. A Technology Assessment of Geothermal Energy Resource Development. Futures Group. 1975.

23. Proposed Geothermal Leasing, Vale Addition. 1975.(TD194 .5 U53 no.10)

24. U.S. Symposium on the Development of Geothermal Resources. Proceedings. 1st,1973; 2nd,1975.

25. The Basis of Applied Geothermal Engineering. By Edward F. Wehlage. 1976. (TJ280.7 W4)

B.  Hydroelectric

Bibliographies

1. Pump Storage, a Bibliography 1961-70. U.S. Bonneville Power Administration. (Z5834 P7 U5 R Sci. Tech.)

2. Pumped Storage for Hydroelectric Power; a Selected List of Reference. Tennesse Valley Authority. 1967. (Z5853 H9 T4 Sci.Tech.)

(For abstracts and indexes see I.A, page 1.)

Statistics

1. Hydroelectric Plant Construction Cost and Annual Production Expenses, 1953-1956. U.S. Federal Power Commission. 1957. (HD9685 U5 A313)

2. Hydroelectric Power Resources of the United States, Developed Undeveloped. U.S. Federal Power Commission. 1960-    . (TJ23 A521) Every 4 Years.

3. Project Independence Task Force Report. Water Resources. U.S. FEA 1974.(HD9502 U52 P76)

4. Water & Land Resource Accomplishments. U.S. Bureau of Reclamation. (HD1421 U5) Annual With Appendices.

Selected List of Periodicals

1. Federal Columbia River Power System; Annual Report. 1946-    . U.S. Bonneville Power Administration. (TC425 C7 A53)

2. The Hydro-Thermal Power Program: a Status Report. U.S. Bonneville Power Administration,Portland. Irregular. 1971-    . (TK1425 B55 A34)

3. International Hydro-Electric System. Annual 1928-    . (HD9685 A1 I6)

4. International Water Power and Dam Construction. IPC Business Press, London. Irregular. 1949-    . (TK1080 W2)

5. U.S. Federal Power Commission. Report. Annual. 1920/1921-    . (HD1694 A4)

6. U.S. Federal Power Commission. Reports; Opinions, Decisions. and Orders. Annual Jan.1931/June1939-    . (HD1694 A45)

Selected Reading Materials

1. Development of Hydropower Engineering in the U.S.S.R. Translated from Russian. By F. IA Nesteruk. 1966. (TK1485 N4)

2. Energy Primer, Solar, Water, Wind and Biofuels. 1974. Portola Institute. (TJ153 E47848)

3. Roman and Islamic Water-Lifting Wheels. Translated from Danish. By Thorkild Schiøler. 1973. (TJ860 S33)

4. Solar Sea Power Plant Conference and Workshop, Carnegie-Mellon University. 1973. Proceedings. (TK1005 S6 1973)

C. Hydrogen and Synthetic Fuels

Abstracts and Indexes

    1. Hydrogen Energy. 1953-1973. University of New Mexico, Energy Information Center. 1974. (QD181 H1 N4 )

       See Also I.A, page 1.

Selected List of Periodicals

    1. Hydrocarbon Processing. (TP690 A1 P4)

    2. Hydrogen Energy.

    3. International Journal of Hydrogen Energy.

Selected Reading Materials

    1. Advanced Coal Gasification System for Electric Power Generation. Multiple-Fluidized-Bed Coal Gasification System Conceptual Design and Cost Estimate. 1975. FE-1514-42.

    2. An Analytical and Experimental Study on the Performance and Emissions of a Hydrogen Fueled Reciprocating Engine. 1974. U.S. Dept. of Trans. Dod-TST Ser.no.74-25. (HE192 .5 U54)

    3. Energy: The Solar-Hydrogen Alternative. By J.O.M. Bockris. 1976.

    4. Hydrogen. Hearings before the Subcommittee on Energy Research, Development, and Demonstration of the Committee on Science and Technology. U.S. House. 94th Congress, 1st Session. 1974.

    5. Hydrogen as an Aviation Fuel. Report Prepared by the Subcommittee on Aeronautics and Space Technology of the Committee on Science and Astronautics. U.S. House 93rd Congress 2nd Session. 1973.

6. Hydrogen as Fuel. National Technical Information Service. 1974. AD-787 484.

7. Hydrogen Economy Miami Energy Conference. 1974. Proceedings. (TP360 H94 1974)

8. Hydrogen Energy Fundamentals. Symposium. 1975. Univ. of Miami, Clean Energy Research Institute, and International Association for Hydrogen Energy.

9. A Hydrogen-Energy System. By D. P. Gregory. 1972. (TP360 C5)

10. Nuclear Heat and Hydrogen in Future Energy Utilization. By L.A. Booth and others. (TK1078 B6) 1973.

11. Prospects for Hydrogen as a Fuel for Transportation Systems and for Electrical Power Generation. (ORNL-TM-4305) 1972.

12. Recommendations for a Synthetic Fuels Commercialization Program; Report Submitted by Synfuels Interagency Task Force to the President's Energy Resources Council. 1975. (HD9502 U52 U62)

13. Selected Topics on Hydrogen Fuel. By W. R. Parrish and others. 1975. (QC100 U565 no.419)

14. The Solar-Hydrogen Alternative. By J. Bockris. 1976.

15. Synthetic Fuels Data Handbook: Green River Oil Shale, U.S. Coal, Alberta Oil Sand. Denver, Cameron Engineers. 1975. (TJ153 H4)

D. Nuclear

Abstracts and Indexes

1. Atomindex. (Superseding Nuclear Science Abstract from July 1976)
2. AEC News Release Index. (QC773 .3 U5 A3 R Sci. Tech.)
3. Meetings on Atomic Energy. (QC770 I55 R Sci. Tech.)
4. Nuclear Science Abstracts. Oak Ridge, Tennessee, Technical Information Branch. 1948-76. (QC173 N8 R Sci. Tech)

   See Also I.A, page 1.

Bibliographies

1. Annotated Bibliography on Atomic Energy; 257 Selected References for schools and Discussion Groups. By Israel Light. 1947. (Z7144 N8 L5 pam R Sci.Tech.)
2. A Bibliography of Current Materials Dealing With Atomic Power and Related Atomic Energy Subjects for Non-Specialists and Lay Persons. By Jane E. Boswell. 1955. (Z7144 N8 B6 R Sci. Tech.)
3. Bibliographical Series. International Atomic Energy Agency. 1960-    . (Z5160 I5 R Sci. Tech. )
4. International Atomic Energy Agency Publications - Catalog. 1972-    . (Z5160 I522 R Sci. Tech.)
5. An International Bibliography on Atomic Energy. United Nations. (Z5160 U4 R Sci.Tech.)
6. List of Bibliographies on Nuclear Energy. International Atomic Energy Agency. 1960-    . (Z5160 I526 R Sci. Tech.)
7. Nuclear Power Economics. International Atomic Energy Agency. 1964. (Z5160 I5 no.13 R Sci.Tech.)
8. Reading Resources in Atomic Energy. Oak Ridge, Tennessee. 1968. (Z5160 U55 R Sci. Tech.)

9. Selected Bibliography on Atomic Energy. U.S. Atomic Energy Commission. 1948. (Z7144 N8 U5 pam R Sci.Tech.)

10. Sources of Information on Nuclear Power and the Environment. U.S. Pacific Northwest River Basins Commission, Power Planning Committee. 1973. (Z5160 U6 R Sci. Tech.)

Directories

1. Sources of Information on Nuclear Power and the Environment U.S. Pacific Northwest River Basins Commission, Power Planning Committee. 1973. (Z5160 U6 R Sci. Tech.)

Statistics

1. Nuclear Power Growth 1974-2000. U.S. AEC WASH-1139. 1974.

2. Nuclear Reactors Built, Being Built, or Planned in the U.S. Office of Assistant General Manager for Energy and Development Programs. Annual. (TID-8200)

3. Operating Experience with Nuclear Power Stations in Member States. Annual. International Atomic Energy Agency. (TK1343 I58)

4. Power (and Research) Reactors in Member States. Annual. International Atomic Energy Agency. (TK9202 I61 R Sci.Tech.)

5. Project Independence Task Force Report. Nuclear Energy. U.S. FEA. 1974. (HD9502 U52 P76)

6. Statistical Data on the Uranium Industry. Annual. U.S. ERDA.

7. Uranium Resources. Production and Demand. Organization for Economic Cooperation and Development. 1972.

Selected List of Periodicals

1. Advances in Nuclear Science and Technology. Irregular. 1962- . (TK9008 A3)

2. American Nuclear Society Transactions. (QC770 A55)

3. Atomic Energy Law Reporter. Commerce Clearing House. 1955- . (KF2138 .15 A6 C6)

4. Atomic Energy Review. International Atomic Energy Agency. 1963- . (QC770 A77)

5. Annals of Nuclear Energy. 1974- . (TK9001 A5)

6. Atomic Data and Nuclear Data Tables. 1973- . (QC173 N74)

7. Nuclear Engineering International. Monthly. 1956- . (TK9001 N877)

8. British Nuclear Energy Society, Journal. Quarterly. 1962-. (TK9001 B77)

9. Bulletin of the Atomic Scientists. Educational Foundation for Nuclear Science. Monthly. 1945- . (HD9698 U5 B8)

10. Current Events: Power Reactors. July 1974- . (TK9001 U55)

11. International Conference on the Peaceful Uses of Atomic Energy. Proceedings. United Nations. Irregular. 1955- . (QC770 I6)

12. International Atomic Energy Agency, Bulletin. 1959- . (HD9698 .5 A3)

13. Journal of Nuclear Science and Technology. Atomic Energy Society of Japan. Monthly. 1964- . (QC770 J66)

14. Nuclear Engineering and Design. (TK9001 N95)

15. Institution of Nuclear Engineers Journal. Institution of Nuclear Engineers. (TK9001 I56)

16. Nuclear Fusion. 6/year. 1960- . (QC770 N78)

17. Nuclear Fusion Special Supplement. International Atomic Energy Agency. (QC770 N78 sup)

18. Nuclear News. American Nuclear Society. Monthly. 1959- .
    (TK9001 N9)

19. Nuclear Safey. Bi-Monthly. 1959- . (TK9152 N9)

20. Nuclear Science and Engineering. Monthly 1956- .
    (TK9001 N94)

21. Nuclear Technology. (TK9001 N82)

22. Nucleonics. L947- . (QC1 N8)

23. Operating Experience With Power Reactors. Conference Proceedings. IAEA. Irregular. (TK9202 C59)

24. Progress in Nuclear Energy. Ser. 8: The Economics of Nuclear Power Including Administration and Law. Irregular. (HD9698 U5 P7)

25. Progress in Nuclear Energy. Ser.10: Law and Administration. 1959- . (TK9153 P7)

26. Report on Public Understanding Of Nuclear Energy. Irregular. Atomic Industrial Forum. Information Bulletin. 1976- .
    (TK9001 A873)

27. Soviet Atomic Energy.

28. Operating Experience: Information on Regulatory Operations Bulletins and Replies. U.S. Nuclear Regulatory Commission. Office of Operations Evaluation. 1974- . (TK9001 U57)

Selected Reading Materials

1. Advanced Converters & Near Breeder. Wingspread Conference. National Science Foundation. 1975.

2. Expansion of U.S. Uranium Enrichment Capacity. U.S. ERDA. 1976. (TD194 .5 U556 no.1543)

3. Fast Reactor Power Stations. British Nuclear Energy Society. 1976. (TK1078 F37)

4. A Fusion Power Plant. National Technical Information Service. 1974. MATT-1050.

5. International Conference on Nuclear Solutions to World Energy Problems. American Nuclear Society. (TK9006 I4764 1972)

6. Nuclear Debate. By Ian A. Forbes, and others. 1974. (TK1078 N75)

7. Nuclear Energy: The Morality of Our National Policy. By William H. Millerd. 1974.

8. Nuclear Fuel Cycle. 1975. U.S. ERDA-33. (TJ153 U535)

9. Nuclear Power and the Environment. American Nuclear Society. 1974. (TD195 E4 A6)

10. Reactor Safety Study. (The Rasmussen Report) U.S. Nuclear Regulatory Commission. WASH-1400. 1975. (TK9152 U53)

11. U.S. Federal Energy Administration. Environmental Impact Statement. ERDA 1500 series. (TD194.5 U5566)

12. Uranium Enrichment, A Vital New Industry. 1975. U.S. ERDA-85. (TJ153 U535)

13. Atomic Industrial Forum. Committee on Fusion. Report. 1976- .

14. Net Energy from Nuclear Power. U.S. FEA. 1976. PB 254-059.

E. Solar

Bibliographies

1. Applied Solar Energy Research; A Directory of World Activities and Bibliography of Significant Literature. Ed. by Jean Smith Jensen.  (TJ810 S8 1959)

2. Bibliography on Domestic and Industrial Applications of Solar Heating. Engineering Societies Library. 1930-50. (Z5852 N37 no. 7 R Sci.Tech.)

3. Heat Bibliography. National Engineering Laboratory, Great Britian. Annual. 1963-   . (Z5853 H27 H4 R Sci. Tech.)

4. Heat and Power from the Sun--An Annotated Bibliography. Heating and Ventilation Research Association.

5. Solar Energy; a Bibliography. ERDA Bibliography Series. 1976. TID-3351-R1P1.

6. Solar Energy and Wind Power; a Selected Bibliography. By Axel C. Ringe. National Technical Information Service. 1974.  (TJ810 R5)

7. Solar Energy Utilization: A Bibliographic Guide. 1976. U.S. Agricultural Research Service. ARS-NE-74 June 1976. (S21 A7694 no.74)

8. Solar Thermal Energy Utilization; a Bibliography with Abstracts. 1974. University of New Mexico. Technology Application Center. Energy Information Center. (TJ810 N4)

   (For abstracts and indexes see I.A, page 1.)

Directories

1. Applied Solar Energy Research; a Directory of World Activities and Bibliography of Significant Literature. Ed. by Jean Smith Jensen. Association for Applied Solar Energy. 1959. (TJ180 S8 1959)

2. Catalog on Solar Energy Heating and Cooling Products. 1975. U.S. ERDA-75.  (TJ153 U535)

3. Solar Directory. 1975-   . (TJ810 S58 R Sci. Tech.)
4. Solar Energy Industry Directory and Buyer's Guide. Solar Energy Industries Association, Inc. 1975.
5. Survey of Solar Energy Products and Services. U.S. Congress. House. Committee on Science and Technology. Committee Print. 1975.

## Statistics

1. Project Independence Task Force Report. Solar Energy. U.S. FEA. 1974. (HD9502 U52 P76)
2. Thermal Energy From the Sea. By Arthur W. Hagen. 1975. Noyes Data Corp. (TK1041 H32)

## Selected List of Periodicals

1. Applied Solar Energy. Bi- Monthly. 1965-   . (TJ810 A7)
2. Solar Age. Monthly. Solar Vision Inc.
3. Solar Energy. The Association for Applied Solar Energy. 1957-   . (TJ810 S6)
4. Solar Energy Digest. Monthly. 1973-   . (TJ810 S613)
5. Solar Thermal Electric Power Systems. Annual. 1973-   . (TJ810 C57)

Selected Reading Materials

1. Conservation and Better Utilization of Electric Power by Means of Thermal Energy Storage and Solar Heating. 1974. (PB-239355)

2. Crop Productivity and Solar Energy Utilization in Various Climates in Japan. Ed. by Y. Murata. (S600 J3) 1975.

3. Energy Primer, Solar, Water, Wind and Biofuels. 1974. (TJ153 E47848)

4. Energy: The Solar-Hydrogen Alternative. 1976.

5. Handbook of Solar and Wind Energy. By F. Hickok. 1975.

6. How to Build a Solar Heater. By T. Lucas. 1975

7. Low Temperature Engineering Application of Solar Energy. Ed. by Richard C. Jordan. 1967. (TJ810 A46)

8. National Program for Solar Heating and Cooling (Residential and Commercial Applications). 1975. U.S. ERDA-23. (TJ153 U535)

9. Optical Methods in Energy Conversion. Society of Photo-Optical Instrumentation Engineers; & University of Rochester, Intitute of Optics. 1975.

10. Optics in Solar Energy Utilization. Ed. Yale H. Katz. Proceedings of a Seminar. (TJ810 O7 1975)

11. Photovoltaic Specialist Conference. Conference Record. Institute of Electrical and Electronics Engineers. (TK2960 P48)

12. Roundtable on Solar Energy. Rockefeller University. 1974. (TJ810 R6 1974)

13. Save Heating Costs; Use Solar Energy. By Keystone Solar Energy Ince. 1975. (TH7413 K49 1975)

14. Sea Solar Plants; a Feasibility Study, Ocean Engineering Design Project. By Robert Arneson and others. (TJ810 S4) 1974.

15. Solar Cells and Photocells Handbook; Theoretical Discussion, Practical Considerations and Illustrated Application Data on the Use of Silicon and Selenium Photovoltaic Cells. 1969. (TK2960 I5)

16. Solar Energy. ASHRAE Journal. Nov. 1975. (TH7201 A53)

17. Solar Energy. H. Messel. 1975.

18. Solar Energy. A Hearing Before the Select Committee on Small Business. U.S. Senate. 1975.

19. Solar Energy and Building. By S. V. Szokolay. 1975. (TH7413 S96 1975)

20. Solar Energy and the Law Workshop. American Bar Foundation, and National Science Foundation. 1975.

21. Solar Energy as a National Energy Resource. NSF/NASA Solar Energy Panel. 1972. (PB-221-659)

22. Solar Energy for Earth; an AIAA Assessment. Ed. by Harrison J. Killian. American Institute of Aeronautics and Astronautics. Ad Hoc Task Force on Solar Energy for Earth. 1975. (TJ810 A6)

23. Solar Energy for Heating and Cooling of Buildings. By Arthur R. Patton. 1975. (TJ810 P37)

24. Solar Energy Home Design in Four Climates. N.H. Harrisville. 1975. (TH7413 T6)

25. Solar Energy in Building Design. N.H. Harrisville. 1975. (TH7413 A6)

26. Solar Energy Projects of the Federal Government. FEA. 1975. (PB-241-620)

27. Solar Energy Proof of Concept Experiments. Mitre Corp. 1973. (PB-231-143)

28. Solar Heated Buildings: A Brief Survey. By W.A. Schurcliff. 1975. (TH7413 S48 1975)

29. Solar Heating and Cooling: Engineering, Practical Design, and Economics. By Jan F. Kreider and Frank Kreith. 1975. (TH7413 K73 1975)

30. The Solar Hydrogen-Alternative. By J. Bockris. 1976.

31. Solar Power Array for the Concentration of Energy. By R.A. Stickley. 1974 (PB-236-247)

32. Solar Primer One: Solar Energy in Architecture. 1975. Bradley Carlson. (TH7413 B7)

33. Symposium on Solar Energy Applications. Papers. American Society of Heating, Refrigerating and Air-Conditioning Engineers, Inc. 1974. (TJ810 S93 1974)

34. U. S. National Science Foundation. Research Applied to National Needs Program. NSF-RA-N series. No. 73-1, 74-13, 74-62, 74-63, 74-90, 74-114, 74-115, 74-119, 74-190, etc. (Q180 U5 U54)

35. A Universal Solar Kitchen. Applied Physics Laboratory. Johns Hopkins University. 1972. (TJ810 S9)

F.  Tidal and Ocean Thermal

Abstracts and Indexes

    1.  Oceanic Abstracts. Ocean Research Institute. Bi-Monthly. (Z6004 P6 O25 R Sci. Tech.)

       See also I.A, page 1.

Statistics

    1.  Thermal Energy From the Sea. By Arthur W. Hagen. 1975. (TK1041 H32)

Selected Reading Materials

    1.  Energy From the Sea: Waves, Tides, and Currents. By Arthur Fisher. Popular Science, May, June, July 1975. (Q1 P6)

    2.  MacArthur Workshop on Energy from the Florida Current. Proceedings. 1974. by Harris B. Stewart.

    3.  Solar Sea Power. Annual Progress Report. NSF-RA-N (74-114 etc.) (Q180 U5 U54)

    4.  Solar Sea Thermal Energy. A Hearing before the Committee on Science and Astronautics. U.S. House. 1974.

    5.  Tidal Power; Proceedings. International Conference on the Utilization of Tidal Power. Ed. by T.J. Gray. (TC147 I58 1970)

    6.  Wave Action in Haleiwa Harbor, Hawaii: Hydraulic Model Investigation, By T.T. Lee and others. 1973. (GC228 H3 L4)

    7.  World Energy and the Oceans. By W.E. Shoupp. 1974. MIT Sea Grant Project Office. Report MITSG 74-7. (GC4 MIT A2)

G. Wind

Bibliographies

1. Energy From the Wind; Annotated Bibliography. By Barbara L. Burke and Robert N. Meroney. (TJ825 B8)

2. Solar Energy and Wind Power; a Selected Bibliography. By Axel C. Ringe. National Technical Information Service. 1974. (TJ810 R5)

(For Abstracts and Indexes see I.A., page 1.)

Selected Reading Materials

1. Applied Aerodynamics of Wind Power Machines. By Robert E. Wilson and Peter B.S. Lissaman. 1974. (TJ825 W5)

2. The Autonomous House; Design and Planning for Self Sufficiency. By Brenda Vale and Robert Vale. (TH7413 V32 1975)

3. Design with Wind. By Douglas R. Coonley. (TK1541 C6) 1974.

4. Energy Primer, Solar, Water, Wind and Biofuels. 1974. (TJ153 E47848)

5. Engineering of Wind Energy Systems. By J.F. Banas. 1975. (SAND-75-0530)

6. Handbook of Solar and Wind Energy. By F. Hickok. 1975.

7. A House for the Future. By Terence McLaughlin. 1976.

8. Progress Report on Research on Wind Power Potential in Selected Areas of Oregon. 1973- . (QC931 O7)

9. Wind Energy Developments in the 20th Century. By Donald J. Vargo. U. S. NASA N75-13380. 1975

10. Wind Machines. NSF-RA-N-75-51. 1975 (Q180 U5 U54 )

11. Wind Power Installations Present Condition and Possible Lines of Development. By Ye. M. Fateyev. 1975.

12. Windmills & Watermills. By John Reynolds. 1970. (TJ823 R48)

13. Workshop on Wind Energy Conversion Systems. Proceedings. 1st, 1973 (TJ825 W52 1973), 2nd, 1975 (Q180 U5 U54 75-50) NSF-RA-N-(73-6) and (75-50).

14. Aerodynamic Performance of Wind Turbines. By Robert E. Wilson, and others. 1976.

15. Wind and Windspinners: A Nuts n Bolts Approach to Wind/ Electric Systems. By Michael A. Hackleman. 1974. (TK1541 H22)

## IV. ENERGY RELATED TOPICS

A. Agriculture and Food Supply

Abstracts and Indexes

1. Application of Modern Technologies to International Development. Quarterly. U.S. AID. (T175 A6)

2. Bibliography of Agriculture. Monthly. (Z5073 U53 R Sci.Tech.)

3. Biological and Agricultural Index. (Z5073 A2 R Sci.Tech.) Monthly except August.

    See also I.A.,page 1.

Bibliographies

1. Agricultural Utilization of Sewage Effluent and Sludge; An Annotated Bibliography. 1968. U.S. Federal Water Pollution Control Administration. (TD760 U5 R Sci. Tech.)

Statistics

1. Agricultural Projections for 1975 and 1985, Europe, North America, Japan, Oceania; Country Studies. Organisation for Economic Cooperation and Development. 1968. (HD1421 O71)

2. FAO Commodity Review and Outlook. Annual. (HD9000 .4 F61)

3. FAO Documentation Center. Index: Statistics. (Z5071 F63 R Sci. Tech.)

4. Monthly Bulletin of Agricultural Economics and Statistics. (HD1421 F61)

5. Production Yearbook. FAO. (HD1421 F62 R)

6. World Agricultural Producation and Trade; Statistical Report. (HD9000 .4 U56) Monthly. U.S. Foreign Agricultural Service. Ceased With Dec. 1975.

7. World Food Production, Demand, and Trade. By Leroy L. Blakeslee and others, 1973. (HD9000 .6 B57)

Selected List of Periodicals

1. Agricultural Engineering. Monthly. (S671 A4)

2. American Journal of Agricultural Economics. 5/year.(S560 J6)

3. American Society of Agricultural Engineers. Transactions. 6 issues/year. (S671 A52)

4. Journal of Soil and Water Conservation. Bi-Monthly. (S623 J6)

5. Agriculture and Environment. June 1974- . (S601 A35)

6. Bio-Science. (QH1 A13)

7. Ceres. Food and Agriculture Organization of the United Nations. 1968- . (HD9000 .1 F2)

8. Organic Gardening and Farming. Monthly. (SB1 O76)

10. Stanford University. Food Research Institute. Food Research Institute Studies. 1960- . (HD9000 .1 S8)



Selected Reading Materials

1. Agriculture and the Fuel Crisis. Hearings before the Committee on Agriculture. U.S. House 93rd Congress. 1st Session. 1973.

2. Balancing Energy and Food Production, 1975-2000. By W.J. Chancellor and J.R. Goss. Science 192(4236):213-218. 4/16/1976.

3. Agricultural Production Efficiency. National Research Council. Committee on Agricutural Production Efficiency. 1975. (S441 N195 1974)

4. Capturing the Sun Through Bioconversion. Proceedings of a Conference. 1976.

5. A Demonstration of Thermal Water Utilization in Agriculture. U.S. EPA. Environmental Protection Technology Series no. 660/2-74-011. 1974. (TD178 .6 A26)

6. The End of Affluence: A Blueprint for Your Future. By Paul R. Ehrlich and Anne H. Ehrlich. 1974. (HC55 E38)

7. Energy, Agriculture & Waste Management. 7th Cornell Agricultural Waste Management Conference. 1975. (S655 C6)

8. Energy, Agriculture & Waste Management. By William J. Jewell.

9. Energy & Agriculture in the Third World. By Arjun Makhijani. 1975. Energy Policy Project of the Ford Foundation.

10. Energy, Natural Resources and Research in Agriculture; Effects on Economic Growth and Productivity for the United States. Economic Research Service. U.S.D.A. 1973. (HD1765 1973 P3)

11. Energy: Sources, Use, and Role in Human Affairs. By Carol E. Steinhart and John S. Steinhart. 1974. (TJ153 S66)

12. The Federal Role in Increasing the Productivity of the U.S. Food System. By G. H. Miles. 1974. NSF-RA-N-74-271. (Q180 U5 U54)

13. Food From Waste. Ed. by G.G. Birch and others. 1976.

14. The Food in Your Future: Steps to Abundance. By Keith C. Barrons. 1975. (HD9000 .5 B17)

15. Food Production and the Energy Dilema. 1974. By Ralph Cummings. (HD9000 .4 C8)

16. Food, Shelter, and the American Dream. By Stanley Aronowitz. 1974. (HC106 .6 A7)

17. Industrial Energy Study of Selected Food Industries. PB-237-316. 1974.

18. Losing Ground: Environmental Stress and World Food Prospects. By W. W. Norton. 1976.

19. Mankind at the Turning Point: The Second Report to the Club of Rome. By Mihajlo Mesarovic and Eduard Pestel. 1974. (HC59 M43 1974)

20. New Look at Energy Sources; Papers Presented at the Annual Meeting of the American Society of Agronomy in Las Vegas. 1973. Ed. by D.E. McCloud and others. (S1 A6 no. 22)

21. Using Power Plant Discharge Water in Greenhouse Vegetable Production. U.S. National Fertilizer Development Center Progress Report. 1975.

22. Workshop on Poultry Processing Plant Water Utilization and Waste Control. 1971 Proceedings. Ed. Roy E. Carawan. (TS1973 W6 1971)

B. Business and Economics

Abstracts and Indexes

1. Business Periodicals Index. (Z7913 B9 R and R Sci.Tech.)
2. Public Affairs Information Service. Bulletin.(Z7163 P8 R)
3. Wall Street Journal Index. (HG1 W21 R)

    See also I.A., page 1.

Bibliographies

1. Energy Crisis in the U.S.: A Selected Bibliography of Non-Technical Materials. 1974. (Z7164 07 C6) Council of Planning Librarians. Exchange Bibliography no.550.

Statistics

1. Commodity Data Summaries. Annual. U.S. Bureau of Mines. (HD9506 U5 U54)
2. Employment and Earnings. Annual. U.S. Bureau of Labor Statistics. (HD5723 A19)
3. Energy Cost of Goods and Services. By Robert A. Herendeen. 1973. ORNL-NSF-EP-58. (HD9544 H4) 1973.
4. Energy in the World Economy, 1850-1975. By Sam H. Schurr. 1960. (HD9545 S3)
5. Energy in the World Economy: A Statistical Review of Trends in Output, Trade and Consumption Since 1925. By Joel Darmstadter. 1971. (HD9540 .4 D37)
6. Energy Prices, 1960-1973. Foster Associates. (HD9564 F67 1974).

7. The European Energy Market to 1980. Staniland Hall Associates. 1975.

8. Growth of the World Industry. Annual. U.N. Statistical Office. (HA40 I6 U4 R)

9. Industry Surveys. Quarterly. Standard and Poor Corporation. (HG4921 S8 R)

10. Organization for Economic Cooperation and Development. OECD Economic Surveys: (by country)

11. Project Independence Task Force Report. Finance. U.S. FEA. 1974. (HD9502 U52 P76)

12. Retail Prices and Indexes of Fuels and Utilities. (HD9540 .4 U48) Monthly. 1955-

13. Quarterly Energy Report for Small Business. National Federation of Independent Business. 1974- .(HD9502 U52 N3)

## Selected List of Periodicals

1. Bell Journal of Economics and Management Science.(HD2763 A2 E4)

2. Business Week. (HF5001 B8)

3. Commerce Today. Bi-weekly.(HC1 C6) Ceased with Dec.1975.

4. Economist. Weekly. (HG11 E3)

5. Energy Users Report. (HD9540 E51 R)

6. Nation's Business. Monthly. (HF1 N4)

7. Public Utilities. Fortnightly. (HD2766 P8)

8. Wall Street Journal. (HG1 W2)

9. Commerce America. (HF1 C612)Supersedes Commerce Today.

Selected Reading Materials

1. Black Gold and Gas Speculation: An Insider Looks at the Risks, Tax Breaks, and Profit Opportunities. By Peter Ronai. 1975. (HG5091 R65)

2. Competition in the U.S. Energy Industry. By Thomas D. Duchesneau. 1975. (HD9502 U52 D8)

3. Economics Aspects of the Energy Crisis. By Harry W. Richardson. 1975. (HD9502 U52 R52).

4. Economic Evaluation of Total Energy: Guidelines. 1973. Decision Sciences Corp. (PB-228-683)

5. Economic Report on Interfuel Substitutability in the Electric Utility Sector of the U.S. Economy; Staff Report to the Federal Trade Commission. 1972. By Thomas D. Duchesneau. (HD9545 D8)

6. The Economic Superpowers and the Environment: The United States, the Soviet Union and Japan. By Donald R. Kelly and others. 1976.

7. Economics of Energy: Readings on Environment, Resources, and Markets. 1975. By Leslie E. Grayson. (HD9502 A2 G7)

8. Energy. By Barry Commoner. New Yorker (AP2 N45). 2-2-76, page 38-66; 2-9-76 p. 38-77; 2-16-76 p.64-103.

9. The Energy Cost of Goods and Services. Oak Ridge National Laboratory. 1973. By Robert A. Herendeen. (HD9544 H4)

10. The Energy Crisis and the Economy. By Walter W. Heller. 1974.

11. The Energy Crisis: World Struggle for Power and Wealth. By Michael Tanzer. 1975. (HD9502 A2 T35)

12. Energy, Ecology, Economy. By Gerald Garvey. 1972. (HC110 E5 G35)

13. Energy: Impact of Availability and Prices on Future Business Prospects. Ed. by David M. Peele. 1975.

14. Energy Prices 1960-73. By Foster Associates. 1974. (HD9564 F67 1974)

15. Energy Resources and Management; Prodeedings. Ed. by
    Joseph T. Zung. 1974. UMR-MEC Conference on Energy
    Resources. (HD9502 U52 U25)

16. Energy Self-Sufficiency: An Economic Evaluation. MIT
    Energy Lab. Policy Study Group. 1974. (HD9502 U52 M25 1974)

17. Energy Taxes and Subsidies; A Report to the Energy Policy
    Project of the Ford Foundation. By Gerard M. Brannon. 1974.
    (HD9502 U52 B68)

18. Financing the Energy Industry. By Jerome E. Hass, J. Mitchell,
    and Bernell K. Stone. 1974. (HD9564 H37)

19. Kilowatt Counter: A Consumer's Guide to Energy Concepts,
    Quantities, and Uses. By G. Friend and D. Morris. 1975

20. The Last Play; The Struggle to Monopolize the World's
    Energy Resources. By James Ridgeway. 1973. (HD9540 .5 R5)

21. Optimal Pricing and Investment in Electricity Supply: An
    Essay in Applied Welfare Economics. 1968. (HD9685 A2 T8)

22. The Poverty of Power: Energy and the Economic Crisis. By
    Barry Commoner. (HD9502 A2 C643 1976)

23. Report to Congress on the Economic Impact of Energy Actions.
    By U.S. FEA. Office of Economic Impacts. 1975.
    (HD9502 U52 U52 1975a)

24. U.S. Economic Development Administration. Environmental
    Impact Statement. (series) (TD194.5 U555)

25. The Use of Econometric Models by Federal Regulatory Agencies.
    By Joe L. Steele. 1971 (HD9581 U5 S8)

26. The World Economic Crisis. By William P. Bundy. 1975.
    (HD9560 .5 B84 1975).

C. Conservation

Bibliographies

1. Energy Conservation and Waste Heat Utilization; a Bibliography with Abstracts. NTIS. 1974. (NTIS-WIN-74-051) (TJ163 .3 L4)

   (For Abstracts and Indexes see I.A., page 1.)

Directories

1. The Energy Activists Directory: Who's Who in Energy Conservation, Conversion, and Alternatives. By John Ross. 1975.

Statistics

1. Project Independence Task Force Report. Energy Conservation. U.S. FEA. 1974. (HD9502 U52 P76)

Selected List of Periodicals

1. Conservationist. Bi-Monthly. (SK351 N44)

2. Journal of Soil and Water Conservation. Bi-Monthly. (S623 J6)

3. Conservation Paper. U. S. Federal Energy Administration. (TJ163.3 U49)

Selected Reading Materials

1. Building for Energy Conservation. Proceedings of a Conference. (NA2542 .3 C6 1973)

2. Citizen Action Guide to Energy Conservation. U.S. Citizen's Advisory Committee on Environmental Quality. 1973. (TJ153 U52)

3. The Contrasumers; a Citizen's Guide to Resource Conservation. By Albert J. Firtsch. 1974. (TJ163 .3 F74)

4. Efficient Use of Energy: (The APS Studies on the Technical Aspects of the More Effieient Use of Energy). Ed. by K. W. Ford and others. 1975. (GC1 A48 no. 25)

5. The Efficient Use of Energy. I.G.C. Dryden. 1975. (TP318 E35)

6. Energy. By Gerard M. Crawley. 1975. (TJ153 C7)

7. Energy Conservation Experiments You Can Do...from Edison. 1974. Thomas Alva Edison Foundation. (TJ163 .3 T5)

8. The Energy Conservation Papers. By Robert H. Williams. 1975. (TJ163 .4 U6 W54)

9. Energy Conservation in Buildings: Techniques for Economical Design. By C.W. Griffin. (NA2542 .3 G74)

10. Energy Conservation Through Building Design and Operation. 25th Annual Air Conditioning Conference. 1976. In: Building Systems Design 73(4), June/July 1976. (TH7201 H38)

11. Energy: Demand, Conservation, and Institutional Problems. Ed. By Michael S. Macrakis. 1974. (HD9545 E58)

12. Energy, from Source to Use. By H. Stephen Stoker, Spencer L. Seager and Robert L. Capener. 1975. (TJ163 .2 S76)

13. Energy: The New Era. By S. David Freeman. 1974. (TJ163 .3 F72 1974)

14. Energy, the Case for Conservation. 1975.

15. Energy: Today's Choices, Tomorrow's Opportunities. By Anton B. Schmalz. 1974. (HD9502 A2 S3)

16. Energy: Use, Conservation and Supply. By Philip H. Abelson. 1974. (HD9502 A2 A2)

17. Fuel Economy Handbook. National Industrial Fuel Efficiency Service. 1974. (TJ163 .3 N3)

18. Joint Strategies for Urban Transportation, Air Quality and Energy Conservation Interplan. NTIS. PB 244-473.

19. Lifestyle Index. By Albert J. Fritsch, and Barry I. Castleman. 1974. (HD9502 A2 F7)

20. Potential for Energy Conservation; Substitution for Scarce Fuels; a Staff Study. U.S. OEP. 1973. (HC103 .7 U51)

21. Saving Fuel. By Robert H. Essenhigh. 1973. (TJ153 E7)

22. Tips for Energy Savers; In and Around the Home, on the Road, In the Marketplace. 1975. U.S. Federal Energy Administration. (TJ163 .3 U5)

23. Energy Conservation Through Effective Energy Utilization. Proceedings of the 1973 Engineering Foundation Conference. Ed. by Jesse C. Denton. Published as NBS Special Publication #403, 1976. (QC100 U565 #403)

24. Energy Conservation Handbook for Light Industries and Commercial Buildings. U.D. Department of Commerce, 1974.

25. Guidelines for Energy Conservation for Immediate Implementation: Small Business and Light Industries. U. S. FPC. Office of the Chief Engineer. (TJ163.4 U6 U5 1974)

26. National Power Survey Practices and Standards: Opportunities for Energy Conservation. U.S. FPC. Technical Advisory Committee on Conservation of Energy. 1974. (TJ163.4 U6 U547)

D. Education

Abstracts and Indexes

1. Education Index. (Z5813 E4 R and R Sci.Tech.)

2. Resources in Education. (ERIC). (Z5813 R4 R)

Dictionaries

1. The Energy and Environment Glossary. Energy and Man's Environment, Inc., 1976.

**Selected List of Periodicals**

1. Intellect. (L11 S3)

2. Journal of Chemical Education. (QD1 J56)

3. Physics Teacher. (QC30 P5)

4. Science and Children. (Q181 S27)

5. Science Teacher. (Q181 S32)

6. Social Education. (H1 S62)

7. Today's Education. (L13 N2)

Selected Reading Materials

1. Resources in Education. Microfiche. (Articles abstracted in ERIC are available on Microfiche)

2. Energy and Man's Environment. Activity Guide. 1976. By Energy and Man's Environment, Portland. OR.. 7 parts.

3. My Energy Book. By Energy Ant. U.S. FEA. 1976.

4. Energy-Environment Materials for School Teachers: Energy-Environment Source Book. By John M. Fowler. 1975.

E. Electricity.

Abstracts and Indexes

    1. Electrical and Electronics Abstracts. Monthly. 1966- .
       (TK1 S3 R Sci. Tech.)

       See Also I.A, page 1.

Statistics

    1. All Electric Homes in the United States; Annual Bills; Cities of 50,000 and More. U.S. Federal Power Commission. Annual. 1963- . (HD9685 U5 A337)

    2. Census of Electrical Industries: 1902- . Electric Light and Power Industry. U.S. Bureau of the Census. 1905- . (HD9685 U5 A32)

    3. Census of Electrical Industries: 1917- . Telephones and Telegraphs. U. S. Bureau of the Census. 1920- . (HE8801 A35)

    4. Consumption of Electric Power in the United States and the USSR as an Indicator of the Standard of Living. Central Intelligence Agency, Office of Research and Reports. 1965. (HD9685 R9 U5)

    5. Electric Utility Cost Units, Transmission Plant. 1948- . U.S. Federal Power Commission. (HD9695 U6 A3)

    6. Electric Output. Edison Electric Institute. Weekly. 1932- (HD9685 U5 E39)

    7. Electric Power Requirements and Supply in the United States, 1940-1945. U.S. Federal Power Commission. 1945. (HD9685 U4 A32)

    8. Estimated Future Power Requirements of the United States by Regions, 1953-1975. U.S. Federal Power Commission. 1954- . (TK1005 U5)

9.  Electric Power Statistics. U.S. Federal Power Commission. Monthly 1937-    . (TK23 A55)

10. Estimated Electric Power Requirements of the United States, 1942-43 - 1943-44. U.S. Federal Power Commission. 1942-43. (HD9685 U4 A321)

11. Gas Turbine Electric Plant Construction Cost and Annual Production Expenses. 1972-    . (HD9685 U5 U54)

12. Historical Statistics of the Electrical Utility Industry. Edison Electric Institute, Statistical Committee. 1962-    . Annual. (HD9685 U5 E41)

13. Industrial Electric Power in the United States, 1939-1945. U.S. Federal Power Commission, Division of Finance and Statistics. 1945. (HD9685 U4 A34 1945)

14. National Electric Rate Book. Rate Schedules for Electric Service in the U.S. in Communities of 1,000 Population or More. Residential, Commercial, and Industrial Services. U.S. Federal Power Commission. 1939-    . Irregular. (HD9685 U5 A2)

15. National Power Survey. U.S. Federal Power Commission. Irregular. 1964-    . (HD9685 U5 A23)

16. National Electric Power Survey. U.S. National Security Resources Board. Irregular. (HD2766 A3 A5)

17. Power Series. U.S. Federal Power Commission. Irregular. 1935-    . (TJ23 A52)

18. Retail Prices and Indexes of Fuels and Utilities. U.S. Bureau of Labor Statistics. Monthly. 1955-    . (HD9540 .4 U48).

19. Rate Research. Rate Research Committee of the National Electric Light Association. Weekly. 1912-    . (TK1 R2)

20. Rate Series. U.S. Federal Power Commission. 1935-    . (HD9685 U5 A3)

21. Statistical Yearbook of the Electric Utility Industry. Edison Electric Institute, Statistical Committee. 1927-    . (HD9685 U5 E4)

22. Statics of Privately Owned Electric Utilities in the
    United States, Classes A and B Companies. U.S. Federal
    Power Commission. Annual 1937-   . (HD9685 U4 A2)

23. Statistics of Publicly Owned Electric Utilities in the
    United States. U.S. Federal Power Commission. Annual.
    1946-   . (TK23 A553)

24. Steam-Electric Plant Air and Water Quality Control Data:
    Summary Report. 1969-   . (TD195 E4 A3)

25. Steam-Electric Plant Construction Cost and Annual Protection Expenses, 1938-1947. U.S. Federal Power Commission.
    1949. (HD9685 U4 A36)

26. Steam-Electric Plant Factors. National Coal Association.
    Annual. 1956-   . (HD9685 U4 N26)

27. Total Electric Utility Industry in the United States Including
    Alaska and Hawaii. Edison Electric Institute, Economics
    and Statistics Division. Monthly. 1932-   . (HD9685 U5 E42)

28. Typical Electric Bills. U.S. Federal Power Commission.
    Annual. 1958-   . (HD9685 U4 A316).

29. World Electric Power Industry. By N.B. Guyol. 1969.
    (HD9685 A2 G8)

30. World Energy Use: Electric and Gas Utility Statistics.
    Pacific Gas and Electric Company. 1959. (HD9685 A2 P2)

Selected List of Periodicals

1.  American Power Conference. Proceedings. Annual.1938-    .
    (TJ5 M5)

2.  E M F Electrical Year Book. Electrical Trade Pub. Co.
    (TK13 E13)

3.  Edison Electric Institute. Bulletin. Monthly. (TK1 E3)

4.  Electric Light and Power; The Electric Service Companies'
    Magazine. Electrical Publications, Inc. 1923-    . (TK1 E53)

5.  Electrical Construction and Maintenance. Monthly. 1901-    .
    (TK1 E45)

6.  Electrical Energy. Monthly. 1956-    . (TK1 E539)

7.  Electricity Distribution; Proceedings of International
    Conference on Electricity Distribution. Institution of
    Electrical Engineers. 1973-    . (TK1 I495 no.99)

8.  Electrical World. (TK1 E56)

9.  IEEE Conference on Electric Heating. Papers. Institute
    of Electrical and Electronics Engineers. Biennial.
    (TK4601 I2)

10. Merchandising Week. Weekly. 1907-    . (TK1 E546)

11. National Electrical Manufacturers Association, Standards
    Publications. Irregular. 1963-    . (TK451 N2 A6 R Sci.Tech.)

12. International Power Sources Symposium, Proceedings. Annual.
    1958-    . (TK1001 I5)

13. Philco Corporation, Annual Report.         1892-    .
    (HD9685 U5 P5)

14. U.S. Federal Power Commission, Reports; Opinions, Decisions,
    and Orders. Jan.1931/June 1939-    . (HD1694 A45)

Selected Reading Materials

1. Cost Considerations for Efficient Electricity Supply. Institute of Public Utilities. By Charles E. Olson. (HD9685 U4 O5) 1970.

2. Electricity Rate Conference. 1974. Electricity Rates and the Energy Crisis. (HD9685 U5 E55 1974)

3. Energy, Electric Power, and Man. By Timothy J. Healy. 1974. (TK1001 H4)

4. Fuel Cell Catalysis Workshop. Electric Power Research Institute. 1975.

5. National Power Survey: Research and Development for the Electric Utility Industry; Report and Recommendations. 1974. Federal Power Commission. Technical Advisory Committee on Research and Development. (HD9502 U52 U58)

6. Optimal Pricing and Investment in Electricity Supply: An Essay in Applied Welfare Economics. 1969. By Ralph Turvey. (HD9685 A2 T8)

7. Perspective on Power: A Study of the Regulation and Pricing of Electric Power. By Edward Berlin, Charles J. Cicchetti and William J. Gillen. (HD9685 U5 B47) 1974.

8. A Procedure for Estimating Non-Fuel Operating and Maintenance Costs for Large Steam-Electric Power Plants. 1975. U.S. ERDA 76-37.(TJ153 U535)

9. Studies in Electric Utility Regulation. By Charles J. Cicchetti. 1975. (HD9685 U5 C53)

10. Towards an Efficient Allocation of Electrical Energy. By Noel D. Uri. (HD9685 U5 U75 1975).

F. Environment

Abstracts and Indexes

    1. Ecological Abstracts. Bimonthly. (QH540 E25 R Sci.Tech.)

    2. Pollution Abstracts. Bi-Monthly. 1970- . (TD180 P58 R Sci. Tech.)

    3. Environmental Abstracts. Monthly. 1971- . (TD172 E48 R Sci.Tech.)

    See Also I.A, page 1.

Bibliographies

    1. Air Pollution Aspects of Emmission Sources: Electric Power Generation - A Bibliography With Abstracts. 1971. U. S. EPA AP-96. (TD883 U34 no. 96.)

    2. Bibliography of Energy and the Environment. Univ. California, Davis. 1972. (Z5853 P83 C3 R Sci.Tech.)

    3. Energy Conservation and Waste Heat Utilization; a Bibliography with Abstracts. By Edward J. Lehmann. National Technical Information Service. 1974. (TJ163 .3 L4)

    4. Energy Recovery from Waste. U.S. EPA SW-36 d.i. and SW-36 d. ii. 1972, 1973. (TK791 U5)

    5. Environmental Quality and Its Control. By. McDonald and K. Hsieh. Oregon State University. 1974. (Z5861 O7 R Sci.Tech.)

    6. Heated Effluents and Effects on Aquatic Life With Emphasis on Fishes: a Bibliography. By E. C. Raney, B. W. Menzel and E. C. Weller. (Z5853 S22 R3 1974 R. Sci. Tech.)

    7. Waste Heat Utilization: a Bibliography with Abstracts. By Axel C. Ringe. National Technical Information Service. 1974. COM-74-10313.

    8. Air Pollution Aspects of Emission Sources: Petroleum Refineries - A Bibliography With Abstracts. 1972. U.S. EPA AP-110. (TD883 U34 no. 110)

Directories

1. Directory of Environmental Information Sources. National Foundation for Environmental Control. 1972. (HC110 E5 N3 R Sci.Tech.)

2. Environment/a List: Directory of Environmental Information Assistance. Oregon State University Extension Service. Special Report 386. 1973. (S105 E22)

3. Environment U.S.A.: A Guide to Agencies, People, and Resources. The ONYX Group. 1974. (TD171 E58 R Sci. Tech.)

4. Environmental Information Systems Directory. U.S. EPA. 1976. (TD173 .5 U52 R Sci.Tech.)

5. Pollution Control Companies. U.S.A. Noyes Data Corp. 1972. (TD173 .5 N68 R Sci.Tech.)

6. World Directory of Environmental Research Centers. 1974. W. K. Wilson, and others. (TD180 D5 R Sci.Tech.)

Selected List of Periodicals

1. Atomspheric Environment. (TD881 A7)

2. Catalyst for Environmental Quality. (S900 C31)

3. Energy & the Environment, Annual meeting. Institute of Environmental Sciences.

4. Environment. (TD180 S3)

5. Environment Reporter. (HC68 E6 R)

6. Environmental Science and Technology. (TD180 E5)

7. Journal of Environmental Education. (S946 E4)

8. Journal of Environmental Health. (RA565 A1 J6)

9. Water, Air and Soil Pollution. (TD172 W3)

10. Water Pollution Control Federation Journal. (TD511 S4)

Selected Reading Materials

1. Air Pollution Control and Industrial Energy Production. By Davis Noll.

2. Ecological Modeling in a Resource Management Framework: The Proceedings of a Symposium. Resources for the Future. 1975.

3. Energy and Environmnet: a Collision of Crises. Ed. by Irwin Goodwin. 1974. (HD9545 E56)

4. Energy and Environment; Methods to Analyse the Long-Term Relationship. OECD. 1974. (HD9502 A2 E54)

5. Energy and Environmental Quality, Proceedings of a Symposium Held May 10, 1974, Illinois Institute of Technology.

6. Energy and the Environment. By John M. Fowler. 1975. (TJ163 .2 F68)

7. Energy, Ecology and the Environment. By Richard Wilson, and William J. Jones. 1974. (TD195 E4 W54)

8. Energy Needs and the Environment. Ed. by Robert L. Seale and Raymond A. Sierka. 1973. (TD195 E4 S95 1971)

9. Energy and the Environment; Proceedings. AIChE Southwestern Ohio Conference on Energy and the Environment.(TJ163 .2 A2)

10. Energy, Ecology, and the Environment. By Richard Wilson, and William J. Jones. 1974. (TD195 E4 W54)

11. Energy-Evironment Materials for School Teachers: Energy-Environment Source Book. National Science Teachers Assoc. 1975. By John M. Fowler.

12. Energy: Resource, Slave, Pollutant. By Robert S. Rouse, and Robert O. Smith. 1975. (TJ153 R69)

13. The Environment--Costs, Conflicts, Action. Ed. by John Cairns and Kenneth L. Dickson. 1974. (HC110 E5 E487)

14. Environmental Aspects of Non-Conventional Energy Sources. Conference. American Nuclear Society. 1975.

15. Environmental Impact of Electrical Power Generation: Nuclear and Fossil. 1975. U.S. ERDA 69-70. (TJ153 U535)

16. The Environmental Price of Energy. Ed. by Alfred J. Van Tassel. 1975. (TJ163 .2 E58)

17. Fisheries and Energy Production: a Symposium. Ed. by Saul B. Saila. 1975. (SH177 E4 F57)

18. Fuel and the Environment; Conference Proceedings, Congress Theatre, Eastbourne, 26-29 November 1973. (TD195 M5 F83 1973)

19. Growing Against Ourselves: The Energy-Environment Tangle. Ed. By S. L. Kwee and J.S.R. Mullender. (TD195 E4 G76)

20. In Command of Tomorrow: Resource and Environmental Strategies for Americans. By Sterling Brubaker. 1975. (HC110 E5 B77)

21. National Power Survey: Environmental Research; The Report and Recommendations to the Technical Advisory Committee on Research and Development. 1974. (HC110 E5 A52)

22. Physical Science; Readings on the Environment. Ed. by Jerry D. Wilson, and Stephen D. Baker. 1974. (TD177 W54)

23. Physics: Energy in the Environment. By Alvin M. Saperstein. 1975. TJ163 .2 S26)

24. Pollution in the Electric Power Industry: Its Control and Costs. By David Logan Scott. 1973. (TD195 E4 S3)

25. Power Over People. By Louise B. Young. 1973. (TD195 E4 Y68 1974)

26. Public Health Risks of Thermal Power Plants; A Report Prepared for the Resources Agency of California. 1972. (TD195 E4 C3)

27. Study of Industrial Uses of Energy Relative to Environmental Effects. PB-237 215. National Technical Information Service. 1974.

28. Thermal Discharge at Nuclear Power Stations: Their Management and Environmental Impacts. IEAE Tech. Rep. Ser. no.155, 1974. (QC770 I56)

29. U.S. Federal Energy Administration. Environmental Impact Statement. (Series) (TD194 .5 U5566)

G. Forestry

Statistics

1. Yearbook of Forest Products Statistics. FAO.

Selected List of Periodicals

1. American Forests. Monthly. (SD1 A5)
2. Forest Industries. Monthly. (SD1 F554)
3. Forest Product Journal. Monthly. (SD1 F565)
4. Journal of Forestry. Monthly. (SD1 J6)
5. Wood'N Energy. 1976- . Society for the Protection of New Hampshire Forests.
6. The Wood Heat Journal. Monthly. 1977?- .

Selected Reading Materials

1. The Complete Book of Heating with Wood. 1974. By Larry Gay. (TH7437 G38)
2. Energy Conservation in the U.S. Pulp and Paper Industry. 1974. (HD9826 S5)
3. Energy Plantations-Should We Grow Trees for Power-Plant Fuel? By R.S. Evans. 1974. Canada. Western Forest Products Lab. Inf. Rep. VP-X-129. (SD433 C37 no.129)
4. Forest Products and the Environment. Ed. by Walter S. Kaghan. American Institute of Chemical Engineers, 1973. (TP1 A52 no.133)

5.  U.S.D.A. Forest Service Environmental Statement. (Series)
    (TD194 .5 U56)

6.  Wood Residues as an Energy Source.  Proceedings.  1975.
    Forest Products Research Society.

7.  Wood Stove Know-How.  By Peter Coleman.  1974. (TH7437 C64)

H. Gross National Product

Statistics

1. Gross National Product. U.S. Agency for Internal Development. Annual. 1967- . (HC79 I5 U55)

2. Handbook of Basic Economic Statistics, for U.S. Only. By Bureau of Economic Statistics, Inc. Annual, Monthly Supplements. (HC101 H2 R)

3. Input-Output Structure of the U.S. Economy. U.S. Bureau of Economic Analysis. 1963- . (HC1 A322)

4. National Accounts Statistics. Organization for Economic Cooperation and Development. Annual. 1957- . (HC79 I5 O6)

5. World Bank Atlas. International Bank for Reconstruction and Development. Annual. 1966- . (HC79 I5 I5)

(For Abstracts and Indexes see IV.B., page 44)

I. Home and Housing

Statistics

1. Project Independence Task Force Report. Residential and Commercial Energy Use Patterns 1970-1990. (Energy Conservation v.1.) U.S. FEA. 1974. (HD9502 U52 P76)

2. Residential Energy Consumption. Report no. HUD-HAI. Hittman Associates. 1972- . (HD9544 H5)

Selected List of Periodicals

1. American Home. Monthly. (NA7100 A5)

2. Building Services Engineer. (TH7201 I5)

3. Building Systems Design. (TH7201 H38)

4. Family Economics Review. (TX1 F3)

5. Heating/Piping/Air Conditioning. May 1929- . (TH7201 H4)

6. Journal of Home Economics. (TX1 J6)

7. ASHRAE Journal. 1959- . (TH7201 A63)

Selected Reading Materials

1. Assessment of a Single Family Residence Solar Heating System in a Suburban Development Setting. By James D. Philips.

2. The Autonomous House: Design and Planning for Self-Sufficiency. By Brenda and Robert Vale. (TH7413 V32)

3. Building for Energy Conservation. Proceedings. (NA 2542 .3 C6) 1973.

4. The Development of a Solar-Powered Residential Heating and Cooling System. U.S. NASA Tech. Brief no. 73-10156. 1973. (TL521 A5391).

5
5. Energy and Housing. A Symposium, Open Univ. Milton Keynes, England. Oct. 31, 1974. Proceedings. Ed. by B.W. Jones. 1975.

6. Energy Conservation in Buildings. Techniques for the Economical Design. By C.W. Griffin. 1974. (NA2542 .3 G74)

7. Energy Conservation Through Building Design and Operation. 25th Annual Air Conditioning Conference 1976. In: Building Systems Design 73(4). June/July 1976. (TH7201 H38)

8. Evaluation of Heating Loads in Old Residential Structures. Hittman Associates. 1974. (PB-227-167)

9. Handbook of Homemade Power. By the Staff of The Mother Earth News. 1974. (TJ153 H33)

10. A House for the Future. By Terence McLaughlin. 1976.

11. Lifestyle Index. By Albert J. Fritsch and Barry I. Castleman. Washington, Center for Science in the Public Interest. 1974. (HD9502 A2 F7)

12. Low Cost, Energy-Efficient Shelter for Owner and Builder. By Egene Eccli. 1976. (TH4815 L68)

13. Other Homes and Garbage: Designs for Self-Sufficient Living. By J. Leckie, and others. 1975.

14. Producing Your Own Power: How to Make Nature's Energy Sources Work for You. Ed. by Carol Hupping Stoner. 1974. (TJ153 S795)

15. Residential Fuel Policy and the Environment. By Alan S. Cohen, Gideon Fishelson and John L. Gardner. 1974. (HD9502 U52 C64)

16. Residential Water Heating: Fuel Conservation, Economics, and Public Policy. By James J. Mutch. 1974. (R-1498-NSF)

17. Retrofitting a Residence for Solar Heating and Cooling: The Design and Construction of the System. U.S. NBS Tech. Note 892. 1975. (QC100 U598)

18. Scientific American Roundtable on Energy Conservation in Buildings. Proceedings. (TK2896 S3 1973)

19. The Sun-Heated Indoor/Outdoor Room for People, for Plants. By Jack Kramer. 1975. (TH7413 K7)

20. Thoughts for the Energy Crisis: The Economics of Insulation and Heating Systems in Typical Willamette Valley Homes. 1974. By James B. Fitch. (TH7216 U5 F5)

21. Tips for Energy Savers; in and Around the Home, on the Road, in the Marketplace. U.S. FEA. 1974. (HD9502 U52 P76)

22. A Universal Solar Kitchen. Applied Physics Laboratory, Johns Hopkins University. 1972. (TJ810 S9)

J. Policy and Politics

Abstracts and Indexes

1. Energy Abstracts for Policy Analysis. U.S. Energy Research and Development Administration. (TJ153 E475 R Sci.Tech.)

2. Federal Register. Index. Contains All Presidential Proclamations and executive orders, rules and regulations of the various Bureaus and Departments of the U.S. Government, and decisions of Fact-Finding Bodies. (J1 A2 Index R)

3. New York Times Index. (AN U5 N72 R)

4. U.S. Code Congressional and Administrative News. Includes all Public Laws, Legislat e history, proclamations and executive orders. (K U544 R)

    See Also I.A, page 1.

Directories

1. Directory of Federal Agencies Engaged in Energy Related Activities. 1975- . (HD9502 U52 D52 R)

Selected List of Periodicals

1. American Academy of Political & Social Science. Annals. (H1 A5)
2. Congressional Quarterly Weekly Report. (JK1 C2 R)
3. Energy Policy. (HD9502 A1 E54)
4. Energy Report. 1975- . (HV8131 E54)
5. Energy Reporter. Mar. 1975- . (HD9502 U52 E492)
6. Energy Systems and Policy. (HD9502 A2 E59)
7. Federal Energy Management Program; Annual Report. U.S. FEA. (HD9502 U52 U539)
8. New York Times. (AN U5 N7)
9. The Progressive. Monthly. (AP2 P75)
10. Science and Public Affairs. Monthly. (HD9698 U5 B8)
11. U.S. Department of State Bulletin. Weekly. (JX232 A22)
12. Vital Speeches. (PN6121 V5)
13. Weekly Compilation of Presidential Documents. (J80 A3 A4)
14. Energy Users Report. Weekly. (HD9540 E5 R)

Selected Reading Materials

1. Beyond the Energy Crisis. By John Maddox. 1975. (HD9502 A2 M33)

2. Energy and U.S. Foreign Policy; a Report to the Energy Policy Project of the Ford Foundation. By. Joseph A. Yager and Eleanor B. Steinberg. 1974. (HD9566 Y34)

3. Energy and World Politics. By Mason Willrich. 1975. (HD9502 A2 W54)

4. The Energy Ballon. By Stewart Udall et.al. 1974. (HD9502 U52 U4)

5. Energy in Perspective. By Jerry B. Marion. 1974. (HD9502 U52 M375)

6. Energy Options in the United Kingdom--a Symposium. Ed. by S. C. Evans. 1975. (TJ163 .25 G7 E5)

7. Energy Policy: Industry Perspectives. 1975. (HD9502 U52 G7)

8. Energy Policy Evaluation; Modeling and Simulation Approaches. Ed. by D.R. Limaye. 1974. (HD9502 U52 W67 1973)

9. Energy Politics. By David Howard Davis. 1974. (HD9502 U52 D3)

10. The Energy Question; An International Failure of Policy. Ed. by Edward W. Erickson and Leonard Waverman. 1974. (HD9566 E56)

11. Future Land Use: Energy Environmental, and Legal Constraints. By R.W. Burchell. 1975. (HT167 F87)

12. A Geography of Energy. By H. Reid Wagstaff. 1974. (HD9502 A2 W33)

13. Handbook of Energy Policy for Local Governments. By Edward H. Allen. 1975. (HD9502 U52 A4)

14. Institutional and Legal Constraints to Co-operative Energy Research and Development. 1975. (HD9502 U52 I6) Prepared by Industrial Research Institute for Commerce Technical Advisory Board.

15. Legislative History on P.L. 93-438: Energy Reorganization Act of 1974. 6 volumes. U.S. ERDA-82. (TJ153 U535)

16. Myths and Realities of the Energy Shortage: Contrivance By the Companies or Bungling by the Government? By Ray E. Storms. 1974. (HD9502 U52 S83)

17. The National Energy Problem. Ed. by Robert H. Connery and Robert S. Gilmour. 1973. (H31 A4 v.31 no.2)

18. Non-Nuclear Futures: The Case for an Ethical Energy Strategy. By. A. B. Lovins and John H. Price. 1975. (HD9502 U52 L68 1975)

19. North American Energy Policy. Ed. by Lawrence Scheinman. 1976.

20. Perspectives on Energy: Issues, Ideas, and Environmental Dilemmas. Ed. by Lon C. Ruedisili, and Morris W. Firebaugh. 1975. (TJ163 .2 P47)

21. Resources and Decisions. By the Leonardo Scholars. 1975. (HD9502 U52 L46 1975)

22. Strategic Energy Supply and National Security. By Carl Vansant. 1971. (HD9540 .5 V37)

23. Studies in Energy Tax Policy. Ed. By Gerard M. Brannon. 1975. (HD9566 B64)

24. Toward a National Policy on Energy Resources and Mineral Plant Foods. By Samuel P. Ellison. 1972. (HD9502 U52 F6 1972)

25. Toward a Rational Power Policy: Energy, Politics, and Pollution; a Report by the Environmental Protection Administration of the City of New York. By Neil Fabricant & Robert Marshall Hallman. 1971. (HD9685 U5 F32)

26. Toward a National Power Policy: The New Deal and the Electric Utility Industry, 1933-1941. By Philip J. Funigiello. 1973. (HD9502 U52 F86)

27. U.S. Energy Policy: Alternatives for Security. By Douglas R. Bohi and Milton Russell. 1975. (HD9502 U52 B63)

28. Unready Kilowatts; the High Tension Politics of Ecology. By Gary Farmer. 1975. (TD195 E4 F37)

29. Resources and Decisions. By the Leonardo Scholars. 1975. (HD9502 U52 L46 1975)

K. Population

Abstracts and Indexes

    1. Population Index. Monthly. 1955-    . (Z7164 D3 P6 R)

Statistics

    1. Census of Population. U.S. Dept. of Commerce. Every 10 Years. (HA201 .19 A5 R)

    2. Current Population Reports: Federal-State Cooperative Program for Population Estimates. Series P-26. 1969-    . (HA195 A56)

    3. Population: Facts and Methods of Demography. By Nathan Keyfitz and Wilhelm Flieger. 1971. (HB885 K43)

    4. Statistical Papers. Series A. Population and Vital Statistics Report. United Nations, Statistical Office. Quarterly. 1949-    . (HB881 U483)

    5. World Almanac. Annual. (AY67 N5 W7 R and R Sci. Tech.)

    6. World Population; an Analysis of Vital Data. By Nathan Keyfitz and Wilhelm Flieger. 1968. (HB881 K4)

L. Social Science

Abstracts and Indexes

1. Essay and General Literature Index. (AI3 E7 R)
2. Social Sciences Index. (H1 S69 R and R Sci. Tech.)
3. Sociolical Abstracts. 5 issues/year. (HM1 S67 R)

Bibliographies

1. Energy: A Bibliography of Social Science and Related Literature. 1975. (Z5853 P83 M62   Sci.Tech.)
2. Energy Crisis in the U.S. : a Selected Bibliography of Non-Technical Materials. 1974. Council of Planning Librarians. Exchange Bibliography. no.550. (Z7164 O7 C6)
3. Environment: A Bibliography of Social Science and Related Literature. 1974. U.S. EPA. Socioeconomic Environmental Studies Series no. EPA-600/5-74-011. (Z7161 M56 1974 R and TD178 .6 A265)

Selected List of Periodicals

1. American Academy of Political and Social Science.Annals(H1 A5)
2. Business & Society Review. Quarterly. (HF5001 B67)
3. Futurist. (AP2 F8)
4. International Affairs. (JX1 I6)
5. U.S. News & World Report. Weekly. (JK1 U6)
6. World Today. (D410 W63)

Selected Reading Materials

1. Human Welfare. Ed. By Barry Commoner. 1975. (HD9502 U52 H84)

2. Energy and Humanity. By M. W. Thing. 1975.

3. Energy and Power. By. W. H. Freeman. 1971. (TJ153 E478)

4. Energy and the Social Sciences; an Examination of research Needs. By Hans H. Landsberg and others. 1974. (HD9502 U52 R4) Resources for the Future.(RFF working paper no. EN-3)

5. Energy: Historical Development of the Concept. 1975.

6. Energy History of the U.S. 1776-1976. So What's New? By U.S. ERDA. 1975.

7. Energy: Sources, Use, and Role in Human Affairs. By Carol E. Steinhart and John S. Steinhart. 1974.

8. Fuels, Minerals, and Human Survival: An Inquiry Concerning the Future of Our Industrial Society. By Charles B. Reed. 1975. (TK9153 R43)

9. Man, Energy, Society. By Earl Cook. 1976?

10. The Social Costs of Power Production: Prepared for the Electric Power Task Force of the Scientists' Institute for Public Information and the Power Study Group of the American Association for the Advancement of Science Committee on Environmental Alterations. Ed. by Barry Commoner. (TD195 E4 S6) 1975.

11. Some Societal Impacts of Alternative Energy Policies. By S. Enzer. 1975.

M. Technology

Abstracts and Indexes

1. ASCE (American Society of Civil Engineers) Combined Index. A Complete Index to All Its Journals, Proceedings and Transactions. (TA1 A498)

2. ASME (American Society of Mechanical Engineers) Transactions Index. A Complete Index to All ASME Journals, Papers and Publications. (TJ1 A52)

3. Applied Science and Technology Index. H. W. Wilson Co. (Z7913 A7 R Sci.Tech.)

4. Chemical Abstracts. Section 52: Electrochemical, Radiational, and Thermal Energy Technology. (QD1 A53 R Sci.Tech.)

5. Electrical and Electronics Abstracts. (TK1 S3 R Sci.Tech.)

7. Engineering Index. Engineering Index. Inc. (Z5851 E57 R Sci.Tech.)

8. International Aerospace Abstracts. Institute of the Aero-Space Science, Inc. (TL501 I55 R Sci. Tech.)

9. Scientific and Technical Aerospace Reports. U.S. National Aeronautics and Space Administration. (TL521 A5409 R Sci.Tech.)

See Also I.A, page 1.

Bibliographies

1. Energy Conversion. U.S. Defense Documentation Center. National Technical Information Service. 1974. (TK2896 U5)

2. Energy Research and Technology - Interim Bibliography of Reports, With Abstracts. National Technical Information Service. 1974. NSF 74-22.

Selected List of Periodicals

1. American Power Conference. Proceedings. (TJ5 M5)
2. American Society of Civil Engineers. Power Division. Journal. (TA1 A496 Sect. 10)
3. Chemical and Engineering News. (TP1 I44)
4. Energy Conversion. (QC621 A3)
5. Engineering News Record. (TA1 E56)
6. Institute of Fuel. Journal. London. (TP315 I6)
7. Intersociety Energy Conversion Engineering Conference. Annual. (TK2896 I5)
8. Journal of Engineering for Power. (TJ1 A52 Ser, a)
9. Power. (TJ1 P6)
10. Power Engineering. (TJ1 P65)
11. Power Engineering - USSR (TK4 P6)
12. Thermal Engineering. (TJ4 T4313)
13. United States. Federal Energy Administration. Technical Report. (HD9502 U52 U537)
14. U.S. Federal Power Commission. Power Series no.1- . (TJ23 A52)

Selected Reading Materials

1. Aspects of Energy Conversion. Science Reasearch Council (U.K.) & Linclon College (Oxford Univ.) 1975.

2. Energy and Man: Technical & Social Aspects of Energy. By M. Granger Morgan. 1975. (TJ163 .2 E46)

3. Energy & Materials. 11th National State of the Art Symp. of the Division of Industrial & Engineering Chemistry. 1975. American Chemical Society.

4. Energy and the Earth Machine. By Donald E. Carr. 1976.

5. Energy Complexes. American Society of Civil Engineers.

6. Energy Consumption in Manufacturing. By John G. Myers. 1974. (HD9502 U52 C66 1974)

7. Energy Technology II: Proceedings of the 2nd Energy Technology Conference. 1975. (TJ153 E4787 1975)

8. Energy Technology to the Year 2000. Technology Review, Mass. 1971-72. (TJ153 E48)

9. The Fires of Culture: Energy Yesterday and Tomorrow. By Carol E. Steinhart. 1974. (TJ153 S67)

10. Flywheel Technology Symposium. 1975. U.S. ERDA 76-85. (TJ153 U535)

11. New Energy Technology -- Some Facts and Assessments. By H. C. Hottel and J. B. Howard. (TJ23 H67) 1971.

12. Reference Energy Systems and Resources Data for Use in the Assessment of Energy Technologies. Associated University, Inc. 1972. PB-221-422.

13. Systems Engineering for Power: Status and Prospects. U.S. ERDA. 1975. (TK1005 S93)

14. U.S. Energy Prospects; An Engineering Viewpoint. National Academy of Engineering. 1974. (TJ153 N24)

N. Transportation

Abstracts and Indexes

1. API (American Petroleum Institute) Abstracts of Refining Literature.
   (i) Petroleum Refining and Petrochemical Abstracts. Weekly.
   (ii) Abstracts of Transportation and Storage Literature and Patents. monthly.

2. Highway Research Abstracts. (TE1 N172 R Sci.Tech.)

3. HRIS (Highway Research Information Service) Abstracts. (TE1 N1717 R Sci. Tech.)

4. Society of Automotive Engineers. Transactions Index. Annual. 1966- . Consists of an Index/Abstract to all SAE Publications. (TL1 S64 R Sci. Tech.)

   See Also I.A, page 1.

Bibliographies

1. Bibliographic List; U.S. Dept of Transportation, Library Services Division. 1969- . (Z7164 T8 U55 R Sci. Tech.)

2. Current Literature in Traffic and Transportation. Transportation Center at Northwestern University. 1961- . (Z7164 T8 C8 R)

3. Electric Automobiles: a Bibliography with Abstracts. By Jeanne Weber Ringe. 1974. NTIS-WIN-74-002. (TL220 R5)

4. A Selected and Annotated Survey of the Literature on Transportation; Status, Structure, Characterisitcs, Problems, and Proposed Solutions. By Jacob Grauman. 1968. (Z7164 T8 G85)

5. Sources of Information in Transportation. Ad Hoc Committee of Librarians. 1964. (Z7164 T8 A3)

6. Transportation: Information Sources; an Annotated Guide to Publications, Agencies, and Other Data Sources Concerning Air, Rail, Water, Road, and Pipeline Transportation. By Kenneth N. Metcalf. 1965. (Z7164 T8 M4 R)

7. Urban Transportation Research and Planning: Current Literature. U.S. Dept. of Commerce. 1945- . (Z7164 07 U8)

## Statistics

1. Automobile Gasoline Mileage Test Results. Annual. U.S. EPA.

2. Census of Transportation. U.S. Bureau of the Census. 1963- . (HE17 A2 R)

3. Energy Statistics: a Supplement to the Summary of National Transportation Statistics. 1974,1975. U.S. Dept. of Transportation. DOT-TSC-DST series. (HD192 .5 U53)no.74-12 & no.75-33.

## Selected List of Periodicals

1. Journal of Transport Economics and Policy. School of Economics and Political Science. 3/year. 1967- . (HE1 J6)

2. Motor Trend. Monthly. (TL1 M6)

3. Transit Journal News. Weekly. 1929- . (TE701 T85)

4. Transportation. Quarterly. 1972- . (HE1 T8)

5. Transportation Engineering Journal of ASCE. American Society of Civil Engineers. Quarterly. 1969- . (TA1 A496 Sect. 16)

6. Transportation and Distribution Management. Traffic Service Corporation. Bi-Monthly. 1961- . (HE1 T85)

7. Transportation Journal. American Society of Traffic and Transportation. Quarterly. 1961- . (HE1 T86)

8. Transportation Research. Quarterly. (HE1 T865)

9. Transportation Science. Quarterly. 1967- . (HE1 T87)

10. Automotive Engineering. Society of Automotive Engineers. Monthly. 1917- . (TL1 S6)

11. Society of Automotive Engineers. Transactions. (TL1 S64)

Selected Reading Materials

1. Automobile, Energy and the Environment. 1975. Harvey Douglas. (TL210 H3)

2. Electrical Vehicle Technology. Machine Design. Oct.17,1974 issue. (TJ1 M15)

3. The Dynamic Environment: Water, Transportation, and Energy. By Edwin H. Marston. 1975. (TC405 M35)

4. Energy and Transportation. Society of Automotive Engineers. 1976. SP-406.

5. Energy: Conservation in Transportation and Construction. Conference Report. 1975. U.S. National Highway Institute.

6. Engine Design to Meet New Social Obligations, 23rd Annual Lectures of Milwaukee Section. Society of Automotive Engineers. 1975.

7. How to Save Gasoline. Public Policy Alternatives for the Automobile. By Sorrell Wildhorn and others. 1975.

8. The Impact of Automotive Fuel Changes on the U.S. Refining Industry; An Economic/Technological Assessment. 1976. U.S. ERDA 76-40. (TJ153 U535)

9. Increased Fuel Economy in Transportation Systmes by Use of Energy Management. U.S. Dept. of Transportation. DOT-TST Series. no. 75-2 v.3. (HE192 .5 U54) 1975.

10. Industrial Energy Study of the Motor Vehicles Industry. NTIS. PB-236 694/6, 1974.

11. Methanol, the Alternative Car Fuel. By John Lincoln. 1975.

12. Per Passenger-Mile Energy Consumption and Costs for Suburban Commuter Service Diesel Trains. NTIS (PB 242-232) 1974.

13. The Role of the U.S. Railroads in Meeting the Nation's Energy Requirements; Proceedings of a Conference Sponsored by the U.S. Federal Railroad Administration. 1974. (HE2717 R6 1974)

14. A Study of the Quarterly Demand for Gasoline and Impacts of Alternative Gasoline Taxes. 1973. Data Resources Inc. (PB-226-132) (HD9566 D3)

O. Waste Recycling

Bibliographies

1. Agricultural Utilization of Sewage Effluent and Sludge; an Annotated Bibliography. 1968. (TD760 U5 R Sci.Tech.)

2. Energy Conservation and Waste Heat Utilization; a Bibliography with Abstracts. National Technical Information Service. 1974. (TJ163 .3 L4)

3. Use of Naturally Impaired Water; a Bibliography. Water Resources Scientific Information Center. 1973. WRSIC bibliography, 200 Series no. 73-217. (TD209 W22 no.73-217 R Sci. Tech.)

4. Waste Heat Utilization: a Bibliography With Abstracts. 1974. (COM-74-10313) NTIS.

5. Wastewater Management: a Guide to Information Sources. Ed. by George Tchobanoglous. and others. (Man and the Environment Information Guide Series, v.2)

6. Water Reuse; a Bibliography. Water Resources Scientific Information Center, 1973- . (TD209 W22 no.73-215 R Sci Tech.)

(For abstracts and indexes see I.A, page 1.)

Selected List of Periodicals

1. Compost Science. (S631 C62)

2. Reuse/Recycle. 1971- . (HD9975 R4)

3. Scrap Age. Monthly. (TS214 S4)

4. Solid Waste Management, Refuse Removal Journal, and Liquid Wastes Management. (TD791 S66)

5. Waste Age. (TD795 W37)

6. Water and Sewage Works. (TD1 M8)

7. Water and Waste Treatment. (TD511 W35)

8. Water and Wastes Engineering. (TD1 W31)

Selected Reading Materials

1. Aluminum as A Component of Solid Waste and a Recoverable Resource. By Ronald J. Talley, and Richard H. Ongerth. (HD9539 A6 T3) 1974.

2. Bioconversion Energy Research Conference. Proceedings. 1973. (TP995 B5 1973)

3. Clean Fuels from Biomass, Sewage, Urban Refuse and Agricultural Waste. Institute of Gas Technology Symposium Paper. 1976.

4. Conversion of Refuse to Energy (CRE). 1st International Conference and Technical Exhibition. 1975.

5. Design Criteria for Mechanical, Electrical, and Fluid System and Component Reliability. U.S. Environmental Protection Agency. Office of Water Program Operations. (TD429 U48) 1973.

6. Design, Operation and Maintenance of Waste Water Treatment Facilities: Federal Guidelines. U.S. F.W.Q.A. 1970(TD429 U5)

7. Electric Power and Thermal Discharges; Thermal Considerations in the Production of Electric Power. Ed. by Merril Eisenbud and George Gleason. 1969. (TK1005 E45)

8. Energy From Solid Waste. By Frederick R. Jackson. 1974. (TD796 .2 J3)

9. Energy from Solid Waste Utilization. 6th Annual North Eastern Regional Antipollution Conference. (ANERAC '75) 1976.

10. Legal and Governmental Structures for Water Management in Metropolitan Areas. 1971. NTIS.(TD223 D4)

11. National Conference on Composting - Waste Recycling. Proceedings. 1971- . (TD785 N38)

12. Power Plants with Air-Cooled Condensing Systems. By E.S. Miliaras. 1974. (TK1041 M5)

13. Practical Heat Recovery. By John L. Boyen. 1975. (TJ260 B67)

14. The Recycling and Disposal of Solid Waste: Proceedings of a Course Organised by the Department of Metallurgy and Materials Science, University of Nottingham. Ed. by M.E. Henstock. 1975. (TD794 .5 R43 1975)

15. Recycling and Disposal of Solid Wastes; Industrial, Agricultural, Domestic. T.F. Yen. 1974. (TD794 .5 R44)

16. Renovated Waste Water; an Alternative Source of Municipal Water Supply in the United States. 1971. (H31 C5 no.135)

17. Resource Recovery From Municipal Solid Waste; a State-of-the-Art Study. 1974. (TD794 .5 N37)

18. Resources. (Renewable and Non-Renewable). Science. 2-20-76 issue. (Q1 S32)

19. Re-Use of Waste Water in Germany. By W. J. Muller. Organisation for Economic Co-operation and Development. 1969. (TD429 M85)

20. A Systems Analysis of the Economic Utilization of Warm Water Discharge From Power Generating Stations; Final Report. By L. Boersma and others. 1974. (TA417 O7 no.48)

21. Thermal Processing of Municipal Solid Waste for Resource and Energy Recovery. By N. J. Weinstein and R.F. Toro. 1976.

22. Total Energy. By R. M. E. Diamant. 1970. (TK1041 D5)

23. Utilization of Waste Heat From Power Plants. By David Rimberg. 1974. (TD429 R55)

24. Wastewater Treatment Ponds. U.S. EPA. Office of Water Program Operations. 1974. (TD429 U485)

APPENDIX I.

## Selected Energy Publications on Oregon and the Pacific Northwest

1. Background Information on Energy Perspectives in the Pacific Northwest and Oregon. OSU Office of Energy Research and Development. 1975.

2. Energy and Raw Material Potentials of Wood Residue in the Pacific Coast States. By J. B. Grantham. 1974. U.S. Forest Service. Gen.Tech. Rep. PNW-18. (SD144 A13 A368)

3. Energy Conservation and Solar Retrofitting for Existing Buildings in Oregon: An Architectural Design Class Project. By J. Reynolds. 1975. Univ. of Oregon.

4. Findings and Recommendations; Final Report. Oregon Legislative Assembly, Joint Interim Committee on Environmental, Agricultural and Natural Resources. Salem. 1974. (KFO 2639 A835)

5. Geothermal Overviews of the Western United States. Compiled By David N. Anderson and L. H. Axtell. Geothermal Resources Council. 1972. (GB1021 G4)

6. Energy in the State of Washington. Energy Policy Council. 1974. Task Force on Energy Profile of Washington(Uses, Sources, and Alternatives). (HD9502 U53 T3)

7. Future Energy Options for Oregon. July 1976. Oregon Dept. of Energy.

8. Geologic Criteria for Siting Nuclear Power Plants in Oregon. 1973. Oregon Dept.of Geology and Mineral Industries. (QE155 N4)

9. Geothermal Environmental Analysis Record, Surprise, Warner and Long Valleys, California, Oregon, Nevada. 1975? (TD194 .5 U53 no.9)

10. Klamath Basin; Environmental Analysis Record for Proposed Geothermal Leasing. Lakeview District, OR. Medford District. 1975. (TD194 .5 U53 no.13)

11. Northwestern Electric Company, Annual Report. 1938-    . (HD9685 U5 N62)

12. Oregon Energy Study. By W. A. Reardon and others. Oregon, Public Utility Commissioner. Salem. 1973. (HD9547 O7 O7)

13. Portland Energy Conservation Project. Reports. City of Portland, Oregon. 1976- .

14. Oregon's Energy Perspective. Oregon, Governor's Task Force on Energy. 1973. (TJ153 O7)

15. An Overview of Energy and Energy Related Research in the West. By Walter Joseph Mead. Natural Resource Committee and Community Human Resource Development Committee. 1975.(HD9502 U52 M4)

16. Pacific Power and Light Company, Portland, OR. Annual Report. (HD9685 U5 P2)

17. Proposed Geothermal Leasing, Vale Addition. 1975. (TD194 .5 U53 no.10) U.S. Bureau of Land Management.

18. Prospectives for Nuclear-Stimulated Geothermal Power in the Western U. S. By Gary M. Sandquist. Western Interstate Nuclear Board. 1973. (TK1041 S3)

19. Review of Power Planning in the Pacific Northwest. Pacific Northwest River Basins Commission, Power Planning Committee. Annual. 1967- . (TJ23 .7 P3)

20. Transition; a Report to the Oregon Energy Council. Oregon, Office of Energy Research and Planning. 1975. (HD9502 U53 O7)

21. Waste Disposal and Environmental Quality in Oregon. OSU Agricultural Experiment Station. 1968. (TD180 A49 R Sci.Tech.)

APPENDIX II.

Selected Energy Publications from Oregon State University

1. Aerodynamic Performance of Wind Turbines. By Robert E. Wilson, and others. 1976.

2. Agriculture and the Energy Crisis. By Emery N. Castle and Ancel D. Haroldsen. 1973. (HD1761 C43)

3. Applied Aerodynamics of Wind Power Machines. By Robert Wilson. 1974. PB238-595. (TJ825 W5)

4. Aspects of Nuclear Power Development and Associated Environmental Protection; Report of a Staff Study Effort at Oregon State University. 1970. (TD899 A8 A7)

5. Background Information on Energy Perspectives in the Pacific Northwest and Oregon. 1975. OSU Office of Energy Research and Development.

6. Citizens Forum on Transportation and the Energy Crisis. 1973. Proceedings. Oregon. State University. Engineering Experiment Station. Circular, no.48. (TA417 072 no.48)

7. Conference on Magnitude and Deployment Schedule of Energy Resources. 1975. (HD9052 U52 C7 1975) Proceedings.

8. A Design Study of an All Year Solar-Energized Residential Air Conditioning System. By Richard A. English. (LD4330 1955 32 MS Thesis)

9. Determinants of Electrical Energy Demand for a State; Methodology and System Simulation. By Warren D. Devine (LD4330 1976D D48 Ph.D. Thesis)

10. Economic Comparison of Alternative Power Resource Development plans in the Lower Mekong Basin. By Pala Sookawesh. 1969. (LD4330 1969 S64 MS Thesis)

11. Electric Power Generation: Comparative Risks and Benefits. U.S.A.E.C. and Institute of Nuclear Science and Engineering. OSU. 1972 and 1973. (TK1078 E5)

12. Energy--A Scientific, Technical and Socio-Economic Bibliography. By Kitty Hsieh. 1976.

13. Estuarine Tidal Hydraulics - One Dimensional Model and Predictive Algorithm. 1974. (LD4330 1974D G66 Ph.D. Thesis)

14. Geothermal Exploration by Telluric Currents in the Klamath Falls Area, Oregon. By Rex Wai-yueh Tang. 1974. (LD4330 1974 T35 MS Thesis)

15. A Guide to Energy Related Terms. OSU. Office of Energy Research and Development. 1975. (TJ9 07 R Sci. Tech.)

16. Information for OSU-OERD Energy Conservation Workshop. OSU. 1975. Office of Energy Research and Development.

17. The Lewis River Hydro-Electric Resource, Its Development and Implications. 1957. By Charles William Booth. (LD4330 1957 9 MS Thesis)

18. Nuclear Power Generation in the Pacific Northwest, a Study. By R. H. Adams, Jr. and others. Oregon State University. 1970. (TK1078 N8)

19. Measurement of Radiant Energy Over a Mixed Water Body. By Paul McAlpine Maughan. (LD4330 1966D 71 Ph.D. Thesis) 1966.

20. A Method of Improving Power System Transient Stability Using Controllable Parameters. 1968. By William Andrew Mittelstadt. (LD4330 1968 134 M.S. Thesis)

21. Power System Engineering and Related Developments in the Northwest U.S.A. 1950. By Tarun Chandra Dowerah. (LD4330 1950 32 M.S. Thesis)

22. Progress Report on Research on Wind Power Potential in Selected Areas of Oregon. Oregon State University. Oregon P.U.D. Directors' Association, Newport, OR. 1973. (QC931 07)

23. Optimization of Staged Rankine Energy Conversion Cycles for High Efficiency. By Larry Dean Simmons. 1973. (LD4330 1974D S586 Ph.D. Thesis)

24. The Role and Policy Implications of Selected External Factors as Applied to the Developmental Patterns of Five Wyoming Fuels. 1975. By Melvin Marvin Vuk. (LD4330 1976D V84 Ph.D. Thesis)

25. Sea Solar Plants; a Feasibility Study, Ocean Engineering Design Project. By Robert Arneson and others. OSU. 1974. (TJ810 S4)

26. A Systems Analysis of the Economic Utilization of Warm Water Discharge from Power Generating Stations. By Larry L. Boersma and others. 1974. (TA417 07 no.48)

27. Thoughts for the Energy Crisis: the Economics of Insulation and Heating Systems in Typical Willamette Valley Homes. 1974. By James B. Fitch. (TH7216 U5 F5)

28. The Use of a Stirling Hot-Air Engine in Converting Solar Energy to Mechanical Power. By Martin Leon Boehme. (LD4330 1962 18 M.S. Thesis)

29. Utilization of Bark Waste. By R.A. Currier, and M.L. Laver. (PB-221-876) 1972. NTIS.

30. Warm Water Utilization. By Larry L. Boersma. 1970. (S594 .5 B7)

31. Wood and Bark as Fuel. By Stanley E. Corder. (Forest Res. Lab. Res. Bull. no.14. 1973) (SD144 O7 A45 no.14)

32. Wood and Bark Residues for Energy. Proceedings. 1975.

33. Wood and Bark Residues in Oregon; Trends for their Use. 1972. By Stanley E. Corder and Others. (SD245 O71273 no. 11) (Forest Research Lab. Res. Paper no. 11)

34. Energy Reference Sources. By Kitty Hsieh. 1975. (TJ153 O75 R Sci. Tech.)

INDEX

Agriculture, 40
Air Conditioning   see Home & Housing
Atomic Power   see Nuclear
Building   see Home & Housing
Business, 44
Coal, 8
Conservation, 48
Economics, 44
Education, 51
Electric Utilities   see Electricity
Electricity, 52
Energy, 1
Energy Conservation, 48
Engineering, 74
Environment, 57
Fluidized Combustion   see Coal
Food Supply, 40
Forestry, 61
Fuel Cell   see Electricity
Gas, 12
Gasoline Mileage   see Transportation
Geothermal, 20
Gross National Product, 63
Heating   see Home & Housing
Home, 64

Housing,   64
Hydroelectric,   23
Hydrogen,   25
Mineral Resources,   10
Natural Gas,   12
Nuclear,   27
Ocean Thermal,   37
Oil   see Petroleum
Oil Shale   see Petroleum
Oregon,   **83**
Oregon State University,   85
Pacific Northwest,   83
Petroleum,   14
Photovoltaic Cells   see Solar
Physics   see Environment
Pipeline   see Natural Gas and Petroleum
Policy,   67
Politics,   67
Pollution   see Environment
Population,   70
Prices   see Business & Economics
Pulp and Paper   see Forestry
Recycling,   80
Sea   see Tidal & Ocean Thermal
Social Science,   72
Solar,   32
Synthetic Fuels,   25
Tax   see Business & Economics
Tax Policies   see Policy
Technology,   74
Tidal,   37
Transportation,   77

Uranium    see Mineral Resources and Nuclear
Utilities    see Business & Economics
Waste,    80
Water Power    see Hydroelectric
Western States,    83
Wind,    38
Wood    see Forestry

Ref
Z
5853
P83
H76

MAR 2 1979

RAYMOND H. FOGLER LIBRARY